Bookpoint 14428 £7-99

D0860610

PSYCHOLOGY
ce

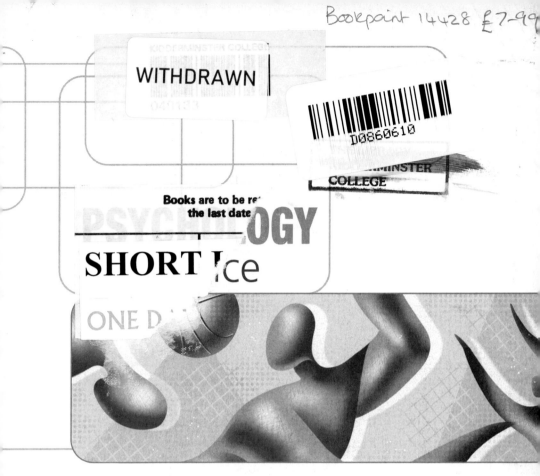

Sport

Barbara Woods

Series Editor: Hugh Coolican

Hodder & Stoughton

A MEMBER OF THE HODDER HEADLINE GROUP

ACKNOWLEDGEMENTS

The author and publisher would like to thank the following for permission to reproduce photographs: Figure 1.3 Action Plus; Figure 2.1 Richard Sellers/Sportsphoto; Figure 3.1 Adam Davy/EMPICS; Figures 3.4 and 5.1 Glyn Kirk/Action Plus; Figure 3.5 Action Plus; Figure 4.4 Human Kinetics; Figure 5.2 Associated Press; Figure 6.1 Action Plus; Figure 6.2 Chris Barry/Action Plus; Figure 7.2 Tony Marshall/EMPICS; Figure 7.3 The National Coaching Foundation; Figures 8.1 and 8.2 Action Plus.

Every effort has been made to obtain necessary permission with reference to copyright material. The publishers apologise if inadvertently sources remain unacknowledged and will be glad to make the necessary arrangements at the earliest opportunity.

Orders: please contact Bookpoint Ltd, 130 Milton Park, Abingdon, Oxon OX14 4SB. Telephone: (44) 01235 827720. Fax: (44) 01235 400454. Lines are open from 9.00 – 6.00, Monday to Saturday, with a 24 hour message answering service. Email address: orders@bookpoint.co.uk

British Library Cataloguing in Publication Data
A catalogue record for this title is available from the British Library

ISBN 0 340 84494 9

First Published 2001
Impression number   10 9 8 7 6 5 4 3 2 1
Year   2007 2006 2005 2004 2003 2002 2001

Typeset by Dorchester Typesetting Group Limited, Dorset, England
Printed in Great Britain for Hodder & Stoughton Educational, a division of Hodder Headline Plc, 338 Euston Road, London NW1 3BH by The Bath Press Ltd.

CONTENTS

Introduction

Psychology in Practice: Sport covers the application of psychology to the sports environment. Although many of us are familiar with terms such as being 'psyched up' for a match or having the 'mental edge' in a competition, in fact, sport is a fairly new area of study for psychologists. This introduction to sport psychology will give you some idea of how it has developed, what it entails and the work that sport psychologists do.

HISTORY

Sport psychology developed in some of the Eastern European nations from the1940s, but did not begin to emerge as a discipline in the US and Europe until the late 1960s. This is when psychological theories and models started to be applied to the sports setting in a systematic way. The first association for sport psychology was the International Society of Sport Psychology, which was founded by a group of European academics in 1965. However, the main focus of academic sport psychology has been in the US.

A major reason for this is the structure of sport in the US, which is grounded in colleges and universities. Inter-collegiate sports are intensely competitive and provide the main springboard for aspiring professionals. Because of this competition, and the readily available pool of participants for sport research, sport psychologists have been able to work with elite performers whilst developing and testing their ideas.

THE INTERNATIONAL CONTEXT

The volume of sport psychology research conducted in the US is reflected in the number of books and journal articles published. This material is naturally biased towards American sports such as baseball, basketball, ice-hockey and American football. As English is the most widely used language for international academic exchange, the material from the US has tended to dominate knowledge about sport psychology.

The balance is now beginning to change as work from other parts of the English-speaking world is becoming widely available. Sport psychologists in Britain, Australia and Canada are reporting on their research and increasingly research from countries such as France, Holland, Italy, and some of the Eastern European nations, is now available in English. Thus, cultural differences are beginning to penetrate sport psychology. Factors such as history, tradition and geography affect what sports are played and people's attitude to them. The recommended reading lists in this book are designed to reflect this wider context. Nevertheless, this still means our knowledge and perceptions are biased towards the West, as work by non-English speaking sport psychologists is still little-known.

SPORT PSYCHOLOGY AS AN ACADEMIC DISCIPLINE

Although sport psychology is now a recognised academic discipline, there is debate about where it belongs. One view is that it should be considered a sub-discipline of psychology, based on the theories, models and research methods of mainstream psychology. Critics argue that this imposes limitations, and you will see that at various points in this book sport psychologists have found difficulties in applying mainstream ideas to the reality of the sport setting. As a result, research over the last twenty years has increasingly addressed the experiences of athletes in the sports setting. This has provided new and fascinating material on topics such as competitive anxiety, self-efficacy, how anxiety and arousal interact in competition, the 'home team' advantage and the use of mental imagery to improve skill learning.

This emphasis on the sports experience is linked to an alternative view. This is that sport psychology should be a sub-discipline of sport science, which also includes motor skills, biomechanics and nutrition. You might find it difficult to appreciate how sport psychology might fit into sport science because these topics are outside the scope of this book. Indeed, the book represents the 'psychology' side of sport psychology. According to the 'sport science' view, the inclusion of sport psychology would strengthen the inter-relationship between sports-related topics and could foster the development of research hypotheses and research methods appropriate to the sport setting.

THE WORK OF SPORT PSYCHOLOGISTS

The topics covered in this book will give you a flavour of some aspects of the sport psychologist's work. It can be loosely divided into the three main areas of clinical, research and educational sport psychology:

- clinical – this involves dealing with emotional or behavioural problems (such as depression or addiction).

- research – this involves establishing and testing theories of sport psychology. We have already noted that this research increasingly has a very practical basis, in other words it is applied psychology.
- educational – this involves helping sports participants and coaches to become more effective. It includes the use of mental skills to improve performance, advice on team building, and enabling coaches to tailor their behaviour to the needs of their athletes.

Generally speaking, the route to becoming a sport psychologist is to have a first degree and then a higher degree or postgraduate qualification. One of these should be in psychology and the other in sport and exercise science.

Barbara Woods

one Personality and sport

As individuals, we have characteristics in common with others, yet we know we are different from everyone else. We call this sense of uniqueness our personality. A key area of debate is whether personality is stable or changes according to the situation. Psychology provides a range of explanations of personality, and therefore a variety of ways in which personality has been measured. We will review this material before considering how personality may be linked to sport performance.

IN THIS CHAPTER WE WILL EXAMINE:

- theories of personality
- measurement of personality
- personality and sport performance.

Theories of personality

The definition of **personality** provided by Richard Gross (1996) is:

> those relatively stable and enduring aspects of individuals which distinguish them from other people, making them unique, but which at the same time allow people to be compared with each other (p.744).

This definition highlights some key questions about personality, which the theories we are going to review will attempt to answer, namely:

- to what extent is personality stable and enduring?
- how can the aspects of personality be identified and measured?
- how and when is personality affected by the environment?
- how is personality related to behaviour (such as sport performance)?

PSYCHOANALYTIC THEORY

Sigmund Freud was the founder of **psychoanalytic theory** and his theory has been developed and re-worked throughout the 20th century. The major features are that unconscious, instinctive drives underlie human behaviour and our personality develops chiefly through the ways we manage them. Freud proposed that personality has three parts:

- the **id** – the 'package' of unconscious instincts (including sexual and aggressive instincts) which need immediate gratification.
- the **ego** – the conscious part of personality which develops as the young child tries to find socially acceptable ways to gratify the id's demands.
- the **superego** – an unconscious part of personality which is related to morality. It stops us from doing things we know to be wrong and judges the ego to see whether it is behaving in a moral way.

Managing the demands of the id in a way which will satisfy the requirements of the superego creates conflict and anxiety which the ego has to cope with (see Aggression, p.25, for details). Freud proposed that people unconsciously use ways of coping with this anxiety, which he called **ego defence mechanisms**. These include:

- **identification** – incorporating someone else into our own personality. Freud's theory is that the child identifies with the parent of the same sex, which is how the boy or girl acquires morals, the sense of being male or female, and other characteristics of the parent.
- **sublimation** – channelling unacceptable impulses into acceptable activities, such as playing competitive sports as a channel for aggression.
- **displacement** – transferring unacceptable feelings about someone or something towards someone or something else which is fairly harmless or powerless and will not retaliate.

TRAIT THEORIES

Two psychologists who saw personality as a core of fairly stable traits were Hans Eysenck and Raymond Cattell. Both used factor analysis, which is a technique for calculating traits which are associated with each other.

eysenck's theory – dimensions of personality

Hans Eysenck (1965) proposed from his research that personality traits can be grouped together in two ways, or dimensions. Each dimension has a biological basis. The first is the **extrovert–introvert dimension** (E) which is related to the level of stimulation we seek and is based on the **ascending reticular activating system** (ARAS). The function of the ARAS is to maintain our optimum level of alertness. The second is the **stable–neurotic dimension**

(N) which is related to emotionality and is based on the **autonomic nervous system** (ANS). The ANS enables us to respond to stressful experiences. Details of these dimensions are shown in Table 1.1.

• **Table 1.1:** The biological basis and characteristics of Eysenck's E and N dimensions

	Biological basis	Characteristics
Extrovert ↑ E ↓ **Introvert**	ARAS dampens down incoming information so the individual seeks additional stimulation in order to maintain a comfortable level of activation.	Becomes bored more quickly. Is less responsive to pain. Seeks change and excitement. Is poor at tasks requiring concentration.
	ARAS amplifies incoming information so the individual prefers low levels of stimulation in order to avoid excessive activation.	Does not seek excitement, prefers calm and quiet. Dislikes the unexpected, prefers order. Is good at tasks requiring concentration.
Stable ↑ N ↓ **Neurotic**	ANS is fairly slow to respond to stressful situations and is not very vigorous.	Even-tempered. Emotionally stable. Easy going.
	ANS responds rapidly and strongly to stressful situations.	Restless. Excitable. Anxious.

Both dimensions are independent of each other, so it is possible to find a stable introvert and a stable extrovert. Particular personality traits are associated with scores on each dimension, as you can see in Figure 1.1 on p.8.

Eysenck (1975) later proposed a third dimension which he called **psychotic** – the strength of the superego (P). The biological foundation for this dimension is associated with the hormonal system and it refers to personality traits related to the individual's relationship or attitudes to others.

An individual can be tested on each of these dimensions using the **Eysenck Personality Questionnaire** (1975), details of which are given in the next section. Most people score on the middle of the E and N dimensions, but score low on P, which indicates a strong superego (showing characteristics such as empathy and co-operation). Those scoring high in psychoticism show anti-social personality traits such as egocentrism, aggression, non-conformity, suspicion, coldness, impulsivity and hostility. Eysenck proposed that some of these qualities are necessary and rewarded in sport, so it is likely that more

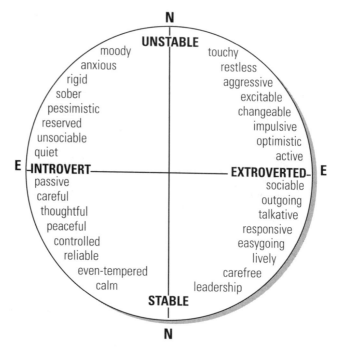

• **Figure 1.1:** Eysenck's dimensions of personality

people with high psychoticism scores are to be found in a sports setting than in the population at large. However the research results are inconclusive.

Eysenck claims that 75 per cent of the basis for these traits comes from genetic influence and 25 per cent from environmental influence. In other words, it is quite difficult to change or modify these personality traits.

cattell's theory – 16 personality factors

Cattell (1965) believed that personality consisted of a number of traits (or **personality factors**). Using factor analysis he identified 16 fundamental personality factors which each of us has to some extent. If an individual completes **Cattell's 16PF questionnaire** (see opposite and p.12 for details), their personality profile can be constructed. The 16 factors and an example of a profile are shown in Figure 1.2

Cattell claimed that the 16PF provides more detailed information than Eysenck's Personality Questionnaire, but he did not claim that individuals will show similar scores each time they complete it. He acknowledged that influences such as mood, motivation and situational factors will affect responses.

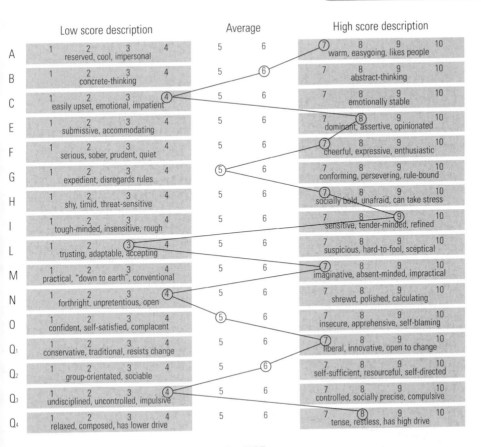

Low score description | Average | High score description

A — 1 2 3 4 (reserved, cool, impersonal) 5 6 7 8 9 10 (warm, easygoing, likes people)
B — 1 2 3 4 (concrete-thinking) 5 6 7 8 9 10 (abstract-thinking)
C — 1 2 3 4 (easily upset, emotional, impatient) 5 6 7 8 9 10 (emotionally stable)
E — 1 2 3 4 (submissive, accommodating) 5 6 7 8 9 10 (dominant, assertive, opinionated)
F — 1 2 3 4 (serious, sober, prudent, quiet) 5 6 7 8 9 10 (cheerful, expressive, enthusiastic)
G — 1 2 3 4 (expedient, disregards rules) 5 6 7 8 9 10 (conforming, persevering, rule-bound)
H — 1 2 3 4 (shy, timid, threat-sensitive) 5 6 7 8 9 10 (socially bold, unafraid, can take stress)
I — 1 2 3 4 (tough-minded, insensitive, rough) 5 6 7 8 9 10 (sensitive, tender-minded, refined)
L — 1 2 3 4 (trusting, adaptable, accepting) 5 6 7 8 9 10 (suspicious, hard-to-fool, sceptical)
M — 1 2 3 4 (practical, "down to earth", conventional) 5 6 7 8 9 10 (imaginative, absent-minded, impractical)
N — 1 2 3 4 (forthright, unpretentious, open) 5 6 7 8 9 10 (shrewd, polished, calculating)
O — 1 2 3 4 (confident, self-satisfied, complacent) 5 6 7 8 9 10 (insecure, apprehensive, self-blaming)
Q₁ — 1 2 3 4 (conservative, traditional, resists change) 5 6 7 8 9 10 (liberal, innovative, open to change)
Q₂ — 1 2 3 4 (group-orientated, sociable) 5 6 7 8 9 10 (self-sufficient, resourceful, self-directed)
Q₃ — 1 2 3 4 (undisciplined, uncontrolled, impulsive) 5 6 7 8 9 10 (controlled, socially precise, compulsive)
Q₄ — 1 2 3 4 (relaxed, composed, has lower drive) 5 6 7 8 9 10 (tense, restless, has high drive)

• **Figure 1.2:** The 16 personality factors in the 16PF

From factor analysis of these 16 personality factors, Cattell claimed there were a number of 'second order' factors, two of which reflect Eysenck's E and N dimensions. Cattell labelled them exvia–invia and anxiety.

SOCIAL LEARNING THEORY

Critics of Eysenck's and Cattell's theories argue that personality traits are not as stable and long-lasting as the theories propose. Cattell himself noted that the same person would give different responses to his 16PF questionnaire at different times, so the profile generated will vary. According to the social learning theorist Walter Mischel (1968), there is little evidence that people behave consistently in a variety of situations. He argued that we see patterns and consistency in the behaviour of others where none exists because we are trying to impose some stability and predictability on our experiences.

   Social learning theory proposes that behaviour is determined more by the individual's situation than by their unconscious drives or biological predispositions. Personality is built up through the processes of **observation**,

imitation and **reinforcement**. As we grow up we observe what other people do, and we may imitate their behaviour. If this imitation is rewarded (reinforced), we are likely to repeat it. Bandura (1977a) proposed that we are more likely to imitate people who are powerful or similar to us, for example someone of the same sex.

Therefore, our personality is built up from our social experiences and from the outcomes of our behaviours. So an athlete may be confident and friendly in a sport setting but shy and withdrawn in a social situation. The social learning explanation for this might be that as a youngster, the athlete imitated successful athletes, experienced success himself and so became confident and outgoing in the sport setting. However, in schoolwork or building friendships he was less successful, he may have used inappropriate models or failed to gain a positive response when he imitated the behaviour of others. This explains why his behaviour is different in a different setting. Critics of this explanation argue that there is more consistency in the individual's behaviour over time and situations than social learning theory suggests.

THE HUMANISTIC APPROACH

Humanists focus on the individual's view of their own experiences and what is meaningful for them. Humanists are concerned with the person's internal experiences, behaviour and their environmental context. A key feature is the emphasis on the human desire for **self-actualisation** – the desire to explore and understand our world, to achieve personal growth and fulfil our potential as human beings.

Maslow (1954) proposed that we have a hierarchy of needs, starting with the basic physiological needs for food and drink. Once these have been met we strive to fulfil higher needs such as those for acceptance, understanding and ultimately self-actualisation.

Carl Rogers (1961) was more interested in the process by which we achieve our potential. He focused on the self, on the kind of person we think we are and the kind of person we would like to be. Essentially the individual needs to feel good about themselves, which Rogers called **positive self-regard.** An example from a sports context would be a swimmer achieving a personal best time. This would increase her positive self-regard.

However, people also need to feel that others approve of them, so they behave in ways which will earn this approval. Rogers termed this **conditional positive regard.** A young cricketer may continue with the sport even though he is not enjoying it, if his participation brings approval from his parents.

Section summary

The theories covered in this section provide different approaches to the definition and understanding of personality. Failure to develop a comprehensive explanation for personality has led to a decline in research. Nevertheless, specific aspects of personality, such as competitiveness, anxiety or aggression, have been studied and their relevance to sport is considered at several points in this and subsequent chapters.

Measurement of personality

A range of techniques have been used to measure personality, including projective tests, interviews and questionnaires. Some examples have already been referred to and are described in more detail below. A summary of some of the issues raised in the use of these measures is given in the Theme Link box at the end of this section.

PROJECTIVE TECHNIQUES

Projective techniques are used by psychoanalysts because they are ways of trying to reveal what the individual's unconscious desires are. Because behaviour is driven by unconscious processes, psychoanalysts are unable to assess personality directly. They have to use indirect methods, such as providing an ambiguous picture and asking the participant what is happening in it. This is known as a Thematic Apperception Test. Even more ambiguous is the Rorschach ink-blot, where the individual is asked to say what they see in the ink-blot.

There are no 'right' answers or scales of measurement in these tests. The individual's responses are interpreted by the tester. This is a major drawback because the tester may be biased and see what they are looking for. In addition, there tends to be a low level of agreement between different testers' interpretations of the same response, so they are low in **inter-rater reliablility**. Essentially, projective tests provide information about motives and emotions rather than personality traits.

INTERVIEWS

Interviews may include closed or open-ended questions. The latter can provide rich and detailed information about the individual (**qualitative data**), for example 'Describe how you feel when you have just lost a crucial game'. In contrast, closed questions require specific answers which make it possible to assess personality traits and make comparisons with others (**quantitative data**). An example would be: 'Which of the following words best describes your feelings when you have just lost a crucial game – anger, shame, or confusion?' However, people may give socially acceptable rather than accurate answers, known as **social desirability**.

PERSONALITY TESTS

Questionnaires are widely used to discover more about human behaviour. Both Eysenck and Cattell devised questionnaires in order to measure personality.

the eysenck personality questionnaire (1975)

The EPQ asks respondents a number of questions requiring a 'yes' or 'no' answer and a score is calculated from the answers. The individual's position on the extrovert–introvert and the stable–neurotic dimensions can then be established. The EPQ includes a Lie Scale which indicates whether people might be giving socially desirable answers. As a way of testing the **validity** of this scale, Eysenck arranged for people who were diagnosed as neurotic to complete the questionnaire. These respondents scored high on the stable–neurotic dimension, which reinforced Eysenck's claim for his scale.

cattell's 16PF

Cattell devised the 16PF questionnaire which measures how much of each trait a person shows. The individual can then be placed at a point on the range 1–10 for each of the factors to give their personality profile, as shown earlier in Figure 1.2. The 16PF has been widely used in research.

Theme link to Methodology

Personality tests are just one kind of psychometric test. ('Psychometric' means measuring psychological characteristics such as intelligence or personality.) These are some of the issues related to the use of tests in psychological research:

- **validity** – the test should measure what it claims to measure. Terms such as personality, extroversion or tender-minded are words for concepts which cannot be accurately defined. Their measurement will depend on an understanding of what the concept means.
- **external reliability** – the tests should produce very similar results every time the individual takes them. Though this appears to be true for Eysenck's test, it is less so for Cattell's 16PF.
- **inter-rater reliability** – the extent to which analysis of test responses are similar. This mainly applies to projective tests.
- **social desirability** – the desire to appear in a good light; may result in answers which may not be accurate or honest.

- **partial information** – personality tests give a restricted picture of the individual, so although they can provide insights into behaviour they do not seem to be good predictors of attitudes, success, motivation or skills, all of which play a crucial part in behaviour.

Methods of measuring personality can be linked to the various explanations for personality. Researchers must be wary of the drawbacks in using these methods, which include interviews, projective techniques and personality tests.

Section summary

Personality and sport performance

Personality research in sport has considered whether particular personality traits are related to the sports which people take up, the positions they take on a team and their success in sport. In this final section we will look at the question: can the elite performer be distinguished from the non-elite on the basis of personality? In reviewing this research you will see how Eysenck's and Cattell's tests have been used.

RESEARCH ON PERSONALITY AND SPORT PERFORMANCE

Elite athletes show distinctive differences in personality profile when compared with athletes of club standard, but these differences are not evident when elite athletes are compared with those of slightly lesser ability. Research by Williams and Parkin (1980) used Cattell's 16PF to compare the personality profiles of

• **Figure 1.3:** The personalities of these speedskaters may be quite similar, according to the research in this section

male hockey players at international, national and club standard. Results showed that the internationals differed significantly from the club players, but the personality profiles of national players could not be distinguished from either of the other two groups.

The personality profiles of world-class athletes are similar to the characteristics of the psychological model for positive mental health, namely low in anxiety, tension, depression, anger, fatigue and confusion, and high in vigour and extroversion (see p.73). This is also true of elite disabled athletes according to Asken (1991), who found they could be distinguished from wheelchair non-athletes on the basis of personality characteristics.

In a review of numerous studies Ogilvie (1968) concluded that eight personality traits were closely linked to athletic performance – emotional stability, tough-mindedness, conscientiousness, self-discipline, self-assurance, trust, extroversion and low tension. This was supported in research by Morgan (1974) who found that athletes were more likely to have stable and extrovert personalities than non-athletes. He proposed that athletes with these personality traits tend to gravitate toward the athletic experience. As they move up the competitive ladder, it is those who are most extrovert and stable who will progress in their sport, whereas athletes with traits which may damage performance are likely to 'drop out'.

This would also explain research by Silva (1984) who found that the higher up the 'athletic pyramid' the athletes were, the more similar their personalities were to others at that level.

However, it could also be that certain traits become more developed as a result of sports participation at higher and higher levels. One study of international athletes found that they were more self-confident, competitive and socially outgoing than non-athletes (Cooper 1969). Does this mean that young athletes with these qualities are more likely to be successful than those without them? Not necessarily it seems – David Hemery (1986) reported that of the 63 international athletes he interviewed, 89 per cent of them said they were initially shy and introverted.

THE INTERACTIONAL APPROACH IN SPORT

This last point returns to the issue raised earlier – are personality traits stable or do they depend largely on the situation the individual is in? Efforts to integrate these two views resulted in the interactional approach, which can explain behaviour more convincingly than traits or situations alone, according to Bowers (1973).

The **interactional approach** focuses on the sporting situation and examines how the athlete's personality affects performance in this situation. This is particularly interesting to sport psychologists because of the extreme situations in which sportspeople can find themselves. For instance they may experience particularly high levels of stress (competition), of boredom (training), of disappointment (losing, injury), of risk (rock-climbing), or of dependence on others (team sports).

The interactional approach takes into account personal factors, the situation in which behaviour occurs and the interaction of these two factors. It predicts that when situational factors are strong, they are more likely to affect behaviour than personality factors. A player who is usually fairly calm may explode with delight on finally winning a close and crucial match. This exhibition is uncharacteristic, a response to this particular situation. However, when situational factors are not strong then personality is more likely to affect behaviour.

The difficulty is – how can situational and personality factors be separated and measured? One technique used by psychologists, known as the **trait–state approach**, has been used particularly to analyse anxiety in sportspeople. This approach is based on the idea that someone who is anxious about many aspects of their lives has the personality trait of anxiety. In contrast, if an individual becomes anxious because of a situation (competing), this is a temporary psychological state.

A performer who has high trait anxiety will experience even higher levels of state anxiety than a performer who is not generally anxious. Ways of distinguishing between trait and state anxiety are discussed on p.56.

THE VALUE OF PERSONALITY TESTS IN SPORT PERFORMANCE

By the early 1980s sport psychologists were divided about the value of using personality tests to predict performance. The credulous view was that, generally, personality tests were accurate predictors of athletic success, whereas the sceptical view was that personality tests were of little value in predicting athletic success.

Theme link to Ethics

The British Psychological Society has produced ethical guidelines and these are applicable to personality testing in the following ways: As personality testing is a sensitive process, testers should not probe beyond what is necessary. The individual must agree to take part in the test and full details of what is involved and the purpose of the test must be explained. Results of the test are confidential and permission must be gained before results can be given to anyone else. The tester should be qualified to administer and interpret the test results.

Morgan (1980) proposes that, taken in conjunction with indicators such as physiological and environmental factors, personality is a useful predictor of motor behaviour. He notes that this relationship is most distinctive in elite athletes, but much less so when athletes of varying ability are studied. In concluding he points out that reliance on a state, trait, or state–trait model is insufficient as a predictor of behaviour because physiological variables play a profound role.

A more extreme position is taken by Cox (1998) who proposes that, in any attempt to explain performance, only 10–15 per cent can be attributed to personality, 10–15 per cent to the situation and a further 10–15 per cent to the interaction between the two. This leaves at least 55 per cent of performance attributable to other factors, such as physical and motor ability. The contribution of all these factors to a full explanation of performance is shown in Figure 1.4.

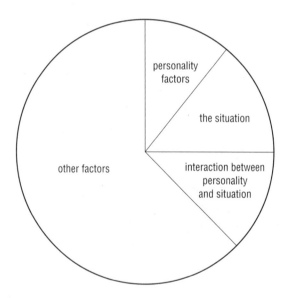

• **Figure 1.4:** The contribution of personality and situation to total athlete behaviour

We have considered the drawbacks in various measurement techniques and the range of debate in relation to the individual/situation explanation for personality. Both of these have contributed to the inconclusiveness of research on personality and sport. In addition, there is considerable variation between sport performers in terms of:

- their level of ability, ranging from the casual social participant to keen club players, county level, national and international level peformers.
- their age, sex and physical fitness.

- the range of sports they participate in, such as table tennis, horse-riding, rock-climbing, skiing, football, squash, swimming, archery, golf, rowing or mountain-bike racing. Sports may be team or individually based, may or may not be competitive and will require a considerable range of physical and psychological abilities.

Section summary

Research on personality and sport performance has failed to identify conclusively the personality characteristics which predict successful performance, although emotional stability seems to be important. Personality profiles of elite athletes do seem to be more similar than the profiles of non-athletes, although we cannot judge whether they develop these characteristics as they progress in sport, or whether they have them to begin with and it is these characteristics which contribute to their success. Overall, personality is seen as only one of several factors which are related to sport performance.

KEY TERMS

ascending reticular activating system (ARAS)
autonomic nervous system (ANS)
Cattell's 16PF questionnaire
conditional positive regard
displacement
ego
ego defence mechanisms
ethics
external reliability
extrovert–introvert dimension
Eysenck Personality Questionnaire
humanistic approach
id
identification
imitation
interactional approach
inter-rater reliablility
observation
personality
personality factors
positive self-regard
projective test
psychoanalytic theory

psychotic dimension
qualitative data
quantitative data
reinforcement
self-actualisation
social desirability
social learning theory
stable–neurotic dimension
sublimation
superego
thematic apperception test
trait–state approach
validity

EXERCISE 1

Which of the theories described has the strongest physiological
element and which has the strongest social element? Explain your
answer.

EXERCISE 2

Describe three difficulties which psychologists have to contend with
when measuring personality.

EXERCISE 3

Describe in your own words a study which has investigated the
relationship between personality and sport performance.

ESSAY QUESTIONS

1. Describe a number of theories of personality.

2. Discuss the value of Eysenck's theory in helping a coach
    improve a sportsperson's performance.

3. Giving reasons for your answer, what advice would you give to a football manager who wanted to select his team on the basis of their personality profiles?

Further reading

Bakker, F. C., Whiting, H.T.A. and van der Brug, H. (1990) *Sport Psychology: Concepts and Applications.* Chichester: John Wiley & Sons (Chapter 3).

Cox, R. H. (1998) *Sport Psychology: Concepts and Applications* (4th ed.). Boston, MA: WCB McGraw-Hill (Chapter 2).

Gill, D. L. (1986) *Psychological Dynamics of Sport.* Champaign, IL: Human Kinetics Publishers (Chapter 3).

Horn, T. S. (Ed) (1992) *Advances in Sport Psychology.* Champaign, IL: Human Kinetics Publishers (Chapter 3).

Morris, T. and Summers, J. (Eds) (1995) *Sport Psychology – Theory, Applications and Issues.* Milton, Queensland: John Wiley & Sons (Chapter 1).

Kremer, J. and Scully, D. (1994) *Psychology in Sport.* London: Taylor & Francis (Chapter 2).

Pargman, D. (1998) *Understanding Sport Behaviour.* Upper Saddle River, NJ: Prentice Hall, Inc. (Chapters 3 and 4).

Wann, D. L. (1997) *Sport Psychology.* Upper Saddle River, NJ: Prentice Hall, Inc. (Chapter 4).

Websites

http://www.wynja.com/personality/theorists.html – useful summaries of some personality theorists

http://www.psychometrics.co.uk/test.htm – information on personality tests and on Cattell

two Aggression in sport

Why are some players more aggressive than others? What effect does the environment have on aggression? Does sport offer an outlet for aggression or create more aggression? Aggression between players, towards officials and by supporters is a constant source of concern in sport. In sports such as boxing or rugby there are behaviours which would not be tolerated in a non-sport setting, yet coaches may use aggression to 'psych up' their players. Clearly aggression has an ambiguous role in sport.

IN THIS CHAPTER WE WILL EXAMINE:

- definitions, types and measures of aggression
- theories of aggression
- reducing aggression.

Definitions, types and measures of aggression

We need to clarify what the word 'aggression' means before we can go on to consider various types of aggression in sport and how it has been measured.

DEFINITIONS AND TYPES OF AGGRESSION

According to Gill (1986), aggression has a number of features. It:

- is a **behaviour** – wanting to hit someone is not aggression, but hitting them is, just as telling them you are going to hit them is also aggressive.
- involves **harm** or injury to another living organism – this can be either physical harm (a cracked shin) or psychological harm (creating fear).
- involves **intent** – harm which is done accidentally is not aggression. If a hockey player comes from behind to tackle an opponent on her stick side and catches the stick on her shin, this is an accident.

From this, we could define aggression as behaviour with the intent to harm another. However, psychologists have distinguished between two types of aggression, depending on the intent behind it, namely:

- **hostile aggression** – the purpose of this behaviour is solely to harm someone, so headbutting an opponent would fall into this category. This is also called **reactive aggression** and is accompanied by anger.
- **instrumental aggression** – here, aggression is used as a means of achieving something, for example tackling hard in order to gain possession of the ball. This is also called **channelled aggression** and is not accompanied by anger.

The rules of a sport define what behaviour is unacceptable or illegal. Of course, some behaviours which are acceptable in a sports setting are unacceptable in a non-sports setting (behaviours in boxing being an extreme example). The term **bracketed morality** is used by Bredemeier and Shields (1986) to describe the temporary suspension of everyday morality in a sports setting. Behaviours that may only be acceptable in a sports setting have been called assertive behaviours by Silva (1980). **Assertiveness** is playing with energy and emotion and within the rules of the game. It:

- is goal-directed to achieve a particular purpose
- is not intended to harm or injure
- uses only legitimate force (even though this amount of force could be called aggression in a non-game setting)
- does not break the agreed rules of the sport.

Officials have to differentiate between assertive and aggressive play. They may have to make immediate decisions about an incident based on what they have just seen, their past experiences, and of course the rules of the game. Whether there is intention or not may be unclear (and well-disguised). Decisions are particularly difficult in sports which involve a high level of physical contact, such as rugby or ice-hockey, because there is greater opportunity for aggression between players. There is also a greater need for discretion on the part of officials who must make decisions.

Just as spectators and participants may disagree about an official's decision on an action, so have sport psychologists. However, they tend to use the decision of the official in order to distinguish between assertive and aggressive behaviour.

MEASURES OF AGGRESSION

Various measures of aggression have been devised, sometimes to meet particular requirements, such as comparing aggression levels in an experimental setting, or assessing aggression as a personality trait. You will see in the next section, Theories of aggression, how psychologists have used some of the measures described below.

behavioural measures

Behavioural measures may be used in an experiment or in observational studies and can include:

- acts of physical aggression towards other people (pushing someone) or towards objects (smashing a tennis racket)
- verbal aggression, such as derogatory remarks or shouting
- punishing another person, either indirectly, such as by the severity of a sentence for someone on trial, or directly, by delivering a harsh noise or even administering electric shocks to another person.

questionnaires

Questions are devised to find out the level of aggression of the respondent, a method widely used to assess aggression as a personality trait. An example is the Bredemeier Athletic Aggression Inventory (Bredemeier, 1978). Questions may also be put to those who know the participant, as a way of assessing their perception of that person's behaviour in their home, social or sports setting.

Theme link to Methodology **(evaluation of methods)**

While it is the most objective and scientific of psychology's research methods, the laboratory experiment is also the most formal and usually the most artificial. Laboratory studies of aggression have, for example, made participants frustrated and then given them the (apparent) opportunity to deliver electric shocks to someone else. This scenario does not reflect most people's experience of everyday life. However, when psychologists use less formal methods, such as naturalistic observation or open-ended interviews, they are unable to exert control over the many variables involved. If they are unable to test the effect of one variable upon another, they cannot draw firm conclusions about cause and effect.

projective techniques

These do not ask the participant directly about aggression, but try to discover what their unconscious feelings are. These are linked to the psychoanalytic approach and are described under Personality on p.11. An example is the

Thematic Apperception Test, in which participants are asked to say what they think is happening in an ambiguous picture. Their answers are analysed to determine the level of aggression which is revealed by their interpretation.

written records

Data relating to the number of violent assaults or aggression-related infringements of the rules may be gathered from police or referees' records.

Section summary The distinction between hostile and instrumental aggression has been reinterpreted for the sports setting to include assertive behaviour. The range of techniques for measuring aggression reflect the needs and priorities of the researcher, who may use more than one method to gain a fuller and more accurate picture. The nature of the research question also influences the type of measure used, as you will see in the research described in the next two sections.

Theories of aggression

In this section we will consider several explanations for aggression. They vary in the extent to which they emphasise innate and environmental factors.

ETHOLOGICAL THEORY

Ethology is the study of animals in their natural environment and ethologists are interested in how animal behaviours increase the animal's chance of survival and the reproduction of the species. Lorenz (1966) argued that aggression is innate. He called it the '**fighting instinct**' and claimed that it was present in all species, and used for survival, enabling members of a species to fight to gain a mate, to protect their territory or to achieve dominance within the group.

All instincts generate a drive or energy which is constantly building up and must therefore be released, otherwise it may be used destructively on other members of the species. Lorenz proposed that animals have evolved ways of releasing excess energy (such as fighting) which are not destructive because they have innate **appeasement rituals**. This means that when one of the pair behaves in a particular way, this indicates submission and the other stops fighting.

Lorenz claimed that aggression fulfilled similar purposes for humans. We are by nature warriors, and participation in sport or exploration provides this 'safety valve' for our aggression. Humans have also devised ways of releasing aggression without destruction. As an example, aggressive behaviour in a competitive sports setting is controlled by rules, referees and acceptable forms of aggression.

PSYCHOANALYTIC THEORY

Freud, in his psychoanalytic theory, claimed that we have instincts which have to be satisfied. Aggression is part of what he called our death instincts, which are destructive. These instincts are in conflict with our life instincts, which are positive and creative. In order that these instincts can be satisfied, they create a drive, so we have to find a way of managing our aggressive drive in a way which is positive, such as by exploring, exercising or sports. These activities are **cathartic**, because they allow the release of pent-up aggression. According to Freud, participating in sports, or simply watching, would reduce aggression.

Freud also maintained that when we want to do something that we know is not acceptable, we cope by using techniques such as **displacement**, which is an ego defence mechanism (see personality, p.6). If the boss makes you really angry you might want to hit him, but you do not. Instead you are very aggressive in your five-a-side match that evening, which is a more acceptable way of releasing aggression. This is an example of displacement – re-directing an emotional response from a dangerous target to a safe one.

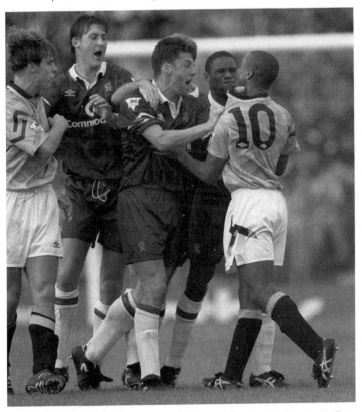

• **Figure 2.1:** Taking part in sport should reduce aggression, according to instinct theories

A key element of both ethological and psychoanalytic theories is that sport should lead to reduced levels of aggression. However, critics argue that this is not generally supported by the evidence, as shown by Berkowitz (1972) who reviewed research in a paper entitled ' Sports, competition, and aggression'. Many have argued that watching sport actually increases aggression, but this may be dependent on the sport. In research by Arms, Russell and Sandilands (1979), some participants watched aggressive sports events (such as ice-hockey and wrestling) and others watched a swimming meet. Those watching the aggressive sports experienced increased feelings of hostility whereas those watching the swimming did not.

THE FRUSTRATION–AGGRESSION HYPOTHESIS

The frustration–aggression hypothesis was proposed by Dollard *et al.* (1939) who viewed aggression as innate, but also saw it as a response to being unable to achieve a goal. The theory is based on the principle of reinforcement, as described in the Theme Link box below.

Theme link to Perspectives (**Reinforcement**)

Reinforcement is a key aspect of **learning theory**, which proposes that behaviour can be strengthened or weakened by its consequences. Anything which strengthens behaviour, which makes it more likely to be repeated, is called reinforcement. After a period of time, the association between the behaviour and the reinforcement becomes well-established. For example, if you think of a tennis player who practises until she has a good forehand drive, the behaviour (making the shot) is reinforced by the speed and accuracy of the ball after it leaves the racket. The player expects that outcome from the shot, so the link between behaviour and outcome is well-established.

Reinforcement can also be used to establish new behaviour. For example, a tennis coach might shout 'good grip' every time the novice uses the correct grip. However, if the behaviour is always followed by reinforcement, learning theory predicts that it will stop when reinforcement stops. To prevent this, reinforcement should become intermittent, once the behaviour has been established. This is **partial reinforcement** and is given only after the behaviour has occurred several times.

The frustration–aggression hypothesis proposes that if the association between the behaviour and reinforcement is broken so that the reinforcement does not occur, frustration results. If the tennis-player slips as she makes the forehand drive and the ball goes out of the court, she will be frustrated and become aggressive. The hypothesis predicts that frustration will always produce some form of aggression and that aggression is always caused by frustration.

This view was thought to be too extreme, and it was soon modified by Miller (1941) who argued that factors such as fear of retaliation, respect for another person, or penalties for aggression might stop someone who was frustrated from actually becoming aggressive. The aggression might be released at a later time (which is related to Freud's notion of displacement), or the individual may instead become half-hearted and withdrawn. This can lead to **learned helplessness** (see p.70).

Frustration is more likely to produce an aggressive response if:

- the individual is close to achieving their goal (the leading skater falls in the final lap)
- frustration is caused deliberately (being tripped whilst dribbling the ball)
- the blocking of the goal is arbitrary or unfair (a bad line-call).

Psychologists using a physiological approach have suggested that one reason why these circumstances are more likely to produce an aggressive response is that the individual is likely to be aroused, and this **arousal** may be redirected when they are prevented from achieving their goal. The next two theories consider the part which arousal plays in aggression.

BERKOWITZ'S CUE-AROUSAL (OR AGGRESSIVE CUE) THEORY

Berkowitz (1969) developed this explanation by arguing that frustration increases arousal, which the individual feels as anger or psychological pain. Anger creates a readiness to act aggressively. However, aggression only occurs if there is a suitable target in the environment. This process is illustrated in Figure 2.2 below.

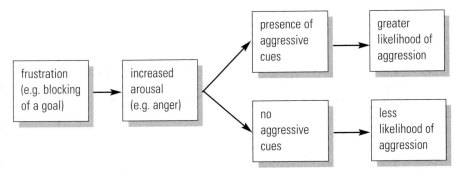

• **Figure 2.2:** Berkowitz's Aggressive Cue Theory

Berkowitz proposed that people learn to associate particular stimuli such as a gun, or a boxing match, or a person with anger or ways of releasing anger. Berkowitz and LePage (1967) found that participants who were made angry showed higher levels of aggression (they delivered more electric shocks) when there was an 'aggressive' cue around, such as a weapon, rather than a badminton racket. In other words, if the individual has learned to associate aggression with particular cues, then the presence of these cues will bring out aggression. Berkowitz illustrated this by saying that although the finger pulls the trigger, the trigger may also be pulling the finger.

Critics of this theory argue that people can be aggressive even when they are not frustrated. Henri Tajfel (1978) suggested that people may be aggressive simply because they are in a situation where aggression is legitimate (for example in sport) or where somebody is seen as a legitimate target for aggression (again, as in sport).

ZILLMAN'S EXCITATION TRANSFER THEORY

This theory focuses on arousal as the key element in aggression. Zillman and Bryant's (1974) explanation is that because arousal takes some time to reduce, it may energise or intensify another behaviour, such as aggression. They created a state of arousal in their participants by having them ride bicycles, producing either a high or a low level of arousal. In the next stage of the experiment they were verbally insulted by someone whilst playing a game. Finally they were placed in a situation where they could deliver an unpleasant sound, via headphones, to this other person. Results showed that those with a high level of arousal delivered more noise.

In a sport setting, there are several elements which will increase arousal in performers. As you will see in Chapter 4, competition can cause arousal because it involves fear of failure, threats to self-esteem, pressure from team-mates and coaches and so on. According to Zajonc (1965), the presence of others, whether as spectators or fellow competitors, causes arousal.

Excitation transfer theory predicts that performers will be in a state of arousal from sources such as these. This arousal may also heighten their levels of aggression, leading from assertiveness (which is acceptable within the sports event) to aggression. Also, an individual who has a tendency to respond with aggression is more likely to respond aggressively in a sports setting because of this arousal.

SOCIAL LEARNING THEORY

According to Bandura's social learning theory, behaviour is learned through **observation**, **imitation** and **reinforcement**. In other words, aggression is not innate, it is learned like any other behaviour.

Bandura, Ross and Ross (1961) selected three groups of 3–6-year-old children. One group played whilst an adult behaved aggressively towards an inflatable doll, another group played whilst an adult worked quietly in the same room, a third group did not go through this stage. Afterwards each child had the opportunity to play with the inflatable doll, and those who had seen the aggressive adult showed higher levels of aggressive behaviour than the other children. Results showed that children imitated these acts, and were more likely to copy behaviour performed by someone of the same sex, or someone who was rewarded.

Core study – Transmission of aggression through imitation of aggressive models

According to Bandura's theory, sport can play a major part in aggression because we observe other people being aggressive, such as in judo, boxing, rugby, football. Having observed a behaviour, we may then imitate it, particularly if it is performed by someone who is powerful or rewarded for their behaviour. Sport provides many examples of people who are the focus of attention, who win trophies, who are cheered by spectators or team-mates. They are influential **models**, so if their behaviour is aggressive it is likely to be imitated. Social learning theory also proposes that we are more likely to imitate those who are similar to us, the same sex, similar age, playing 'our' sport.

This brings us to the role of the media, which provides many more models than an individual would see in the flesh. Imagine a young soccer player who is watching a match on TV. If he observes a top player shouting and gesturing at the referee, the youngster may copy the model's behaviour in his own matches. The way sportspeople are presented, which behaviours are broadcast, the attitudes of sports commentators and what is 'newsworthy' all help to shape the viewer's perceptions and behaviours.

The theories of aggression which we have reviewed offer various explanations for human aggression. Some common themes emerge, such as the role of arousal, the influence of environmental factors in creating and directing aggression, and the view that aggression is based on factors which are innate. Although there is no agreed explanation for aggression, these theories are useful because they suggest ways in which aggression can be reduced, which is the final topic in this chapter.

Section summary

Reducing aggression

From the explanations described above, you will see that there are two conflicting views of the role of sport in aggression. One is that sport teaches people how to be aggressive, creates situations which increase aggression, and provides opportunities and rewards for being aggressive. The opposing view is that sport offers an outlet for aggression and an opportunity to learn how to control it.

If you agree with the first view, then sport should be discouraged, whereas according to the second view it should be encouraged. Of course nothing is ever this simple and there is some value in both views. In addition, given the social and health benefits of sport participation (see exercise and health, p.72), concern has focused on how aggression in sport can be reduced. Methods for reducing aggression can be classed as behavioural or cognitive.

BEHAVIOURAL TECHNIQUES

We have already come across aspects of **learning theory** in this chapter. Reinforcement (described on p.26) is anything which makes behaviour more likely to be repeated, and social learning theory proposes that behaviour is learned through imitation of models. Another element of learning theory is **punishment**, which is anything which makes behaviour less likely to happen. As you can see below, behavioural techniques for reducing aggression are based on these principles. For example:

- reward non-aggressive behaviour – sportspeople who show non-aggressive behaviour (or show that they are controlling their aggression) should be praised and publicised.
- provide non-aggressive models – sports participants should remember that they are role models for others, and should be applauded when they act as models of desirable sporting behaviour.
- penalise those who show aggression – punishment such as penalties, fines, disapproval or suspension should be applied to those who display or encourage aggression, whether they are players, coaches or spectators.

COGNITIVE INTERVENTIONS

Whilst some behavioural techniques may reduce aggression, they depend on other people trying to change an individual's behaviour. Cognitive psychologists criticise learning theory because it focuses on the individual's behaviour, rather than on their understanding and motivation. The focus in **cognitive psychology** is our thinking, and how it affects our behaviour. For example, a player is more likely to retaliate aggressively if he thinks a hard tackle is intentional rather than accidental.

Cognitive interventions are designed to help players change the way they think about situations so that they can change their behaviour. For example, a player may retaliate after a tackle because he interprets it as intended to harm him. If he can be encouraged to see the opposing player as simply following his manager's instructions, he may be less likely to retaliate.

Self-talk can be employed to direct thoughts or actions. You will see how this is used in the examples of cognitive interventions described below:

- substituting negative thoughts with positive ones – so when a referee gives a poor decision, the negative thoughts ('there's no way that was off-side...') are replaced by positive ones ('right, get the ball back, take them by surprise').
- breaking the habit of an aggressive response – as soon as players feel aggression increasing they say 'Stop!'
- rewarding non-aggressive behaviour – when players succeed in curbing their aggressive feelings they congratulate themselves.
- changing the focus of attention – the player shifts attention to another aspect of the situation ('watch for the short pass') in order to distract themselves from the aggressive stimulus.
- reducing arousal and controlling emotions by relaxation – 'Ok now, d..e..e..p breath'
- using **performance-related goals** rather than **outcome-related goals** – athletes remind themselves of the particular goals they must achieve during the sports activity so that they do not become distracted by the opposition's performance or the likelihood of losing.

Section summary

By its very nature, the sport setting makes aggression more likely, and sometimes rewards it. There are also ways of reducing the aggression we experience as individuals, in or out of sport. This section has shown how anyone involved in sport can provide reinforcement or punishment for the behaviour of others and may be a model for the behaviour of others. However, we are each responsible for our own actions and under the cognitive heading we considered ways in which we can reduce the likelihood of an aggressive response by changing the way we understand our experiences.

KEY TERMS

aggressive-cue theory
appeasement rituals
arousal
assertiveness
bracketed morality
channelled aggression
cognitive psychology
cue arousal
displacement
ethological theory
excitation transfer theory
fighting instinct
formal research methods
frustration–aggression hypothesis
hostile aggression
imitation
instrumental aggression
learned helplessness
learning theory
models
observational
outcome-related goals
partial reinforcement
performance-related goals
psychoanalytic theory
punishment
reactive aggression
reinforcement
self-talk
social learning theory

EXERCISE **1**

Working in pairs, first choose a sport. Individually, think of one
example of assertiveness and one of aggression in that sport. Then
discuss your examples with your partner and decide whether all
four examples are good ones.

EXERCISE 2

Describe and evaluate a laboratory experiment on aggression which is mentioned in this chapter.

EXERCISE 3

In a group, decide on an example of aggression in a sport setting. Individually, plan how you would reduce it. Get together with the others and compare your proposals. Which one do you think has the best chance of success?

ESSAY QUESTIONS

1. Describe the part which arousal plays in aggression.

2. Discuss two theories of aggression, saying which provides the best explanation for aggression in sport. Justify your answer by comparing and evaluating both theories.

3. Describe a behavioural and a cognitive method for reducing aggression in sport. Consider some of the reasons why they may be difficult to put into practice.

Further reading

Bakker, F. C., Whiting, H. T. A. and van der Brug, H. (1990) *Sport Psychology: Concepts and Applications*. Chichester: John Wiley & Sons (Chapter 4).

Cox, R. H. (1998) *Sport Psychology: Concepts and Applications* (4th ed.). Boston, MA: WCB McGraw-Hill (Chapter 9).

Gill, D. L. (1986) *Psychological Dynamics of Sport*. Champaign, IL: Human Kinetics Publishers (Chapter 12).

Kremer, J. and Scully, D. (1994) *Psychology in Sport*. London: Taylor & Francis (Chapter 6).

Pargman, D. (1998) *Understanding Sport Behaviour*. Upper Saddle River, NJ: Prentice Hall, Inc. (Chapter 8).

Wann, D. L. (1997) *Sport Psychology*. Upper Saddle River, NJ: Prentice Hall, Inc. (Chapter 12).

Websites

http://www.calstatela.edu/faculty/dfrankl/soccer/violence.htm – background to causes of aggression in sport and ways of reducing it.

news.bbc.co.uk/sport/hi/english/funny_old_game/newsid_1494000/1494252. stm – some up-to-the-minute quotations and data on aggression in sport.

3 Motivation and self-confidence in sport

Why do people work to improve their skills? Why do marathon runners continue despite pain? In other words, what motivates people to persist at something which is time-consuming, painful or brings failure? A related aspect of motivation is self-confidence, the belief that we can tackle all kinds of challenges and succeed. Such belief is a considerable asset to the sportsperson.

IN THIS CHAPTER WE WILL EXAMINE:

- definitions and models of motivation
- models of self-confidence
- improving motivation and self-confidence.

Definitions and models of motivation

Motivation can be defined as a drive to fulfil a need. Gill (1986) noted that it drives us to do things (it energises our behaviour) and it makes us do particular things (it directs our behaviour). Some psychologists have seen arousal as the basis for motivation, and arousal is discussed in detail in Chapter 4. Here we will examine motivation as a personality trait.

ACHIEVEMENT MOTIVATION – THE McCLELLAND-ATKINSON MODEL

Imagine a young footballer in the last five minutes of a game where the score is 1–1: he is asked if he wants to take the penalty kick. He considers he has a fifty–fifty chance of failing, imagines the shame of doing so and says 'No thanks'. His behaviour is driven by the **motive to avoid failure**. The next player who is asked thinks 'Hey, this is my chance to be a hero, I can save the match' and takes the penalty kick. He is driven by the **motive to achieve success**.

The McClelland-Atkinson (1953) model of **achievement motivation** is based on the two motives described above. It must be noted that these motives are not directly measurable as they are theoretical concepts, not observable events. Nevertheless McClelland, Atkinson, Clark and Lowell (1953) reported that those with a high motive to achieve are more likely to:

- show high levels of performance
- persist for longer and value feedback from others
- attribute their performance to internal factors such as effort (for more on attribution see Chapter 5).

In contrast, those with a high motive to avoid failure tend to avoid tasks in which they can be evaluated by others or at which they might fail. They tend to attribute their successes to external factors such as luck. Although everyone has these two motives to some extent, it is the difference between them which provides the personality factor called achievement motivation. The greater the difference, the higher the achievement motivation.

This model also considers the situation for the individual. If you recall our two young footballers, they viewed the fifty–fifty chance of scoring a penalty kick in different ways. There were two aspects to the task which determined their behaviour:

• **Figure 3.1:** Newcastle Falcon's Jonny Wilkinson positions the ball for a penalty kick.

- **task difficulty** – the probability of success or of failure in the task
- **incentive value of success** – the importance to the individual of success or failure in the task.

According to this model, high achievers would prefer to do a task with a fifty–fifty chance of success, such as playing an opponent of similar ability. The low achiever has a strong motive to avoid failure, so would prefer to play against a very weak opponent (guaranteed success) or a very strong opponent (no-one would blame him for failing). Ideally, the low achiever prefers to avoid all challenges.

Critics of this model argue that these concepts are difficult to test, that it is not useful for people who have a moderate score on both measures, and that factors such as reinforcement should also be considered (see extrinsic motivation later in this chapter, p.41). Evidence from research is mixed, for example Fodero's (1980) study of elite gymnasts failed to find a relationship between their achievement motivation and performance. Another point is that achievement motivation should not be seen as a 'global' concept but as related to particular situations. This has led sport psychologists to talk of sport-specific achievement motivation – in other words, competitiveness.

COMPETITIVENESS – SPORT-SPECIFIC ACHIEVEMENT MOTIVATION

Competitiveness has been defined by Gill (1986) as a sport-specific form of achievement motivation. She developed the **Sport Orientation Questionnaire** (Gill and Deeter 1988) in order to measure three aspects of achievement in sport. It comprises 25 items which together assess:

- **competitiveness** – the desire to seek and strive for success in sport-specific situations.
- **win orientation** – the desire to win interpersonal competitive sporting events (sometimes called **outcome orientation**). The athlete judges her success compared to others, but because the outcome of competition is unpredictable and outside her control, the win oriented athlete may have difficulty maintaining a feeling of competence after several failures and be less likely to remain motivated. To protect her self-worth she may choose to play in situations where she is bound to win or bound to fail.
- **goal orientation** – the desire to reach personal goals in sport (sometimes called **performance** or **task orientation**). The goal oriented athlete focuses on her own performance, sets personal goals and aims to improve her performance from the previous time. She is likely to feel in control and to choose realistic tasks and opponents. She is also less likely to feel that losing is a major setback and so is more persistent and does not fear failure.

Research by Gill and Dzewaltowski (1988) used the SOQ to compare athletes and non-athletes, and male and female athletes. Results showed that athletes scored higher than non-athletes on most dimensions of the SOQ, and that they were more concerned about performance and less about outcome than non-athletes.

Section summary This section has examined achievement motivation, which is seen as a stable disposition and is indicated by the individual's attitude to tasks which have a fifty–fifty chance of success. This has been applied to a sport setting, where it is known as sport-specific achievement motivation. This can be assessed by using the SOQ.

Models of self-confidence

Interest in the McClelland-Atkinson model declined as research into self-confidence increased during the late 1970s. This research proposed that self-confidence is what distinguishes the person who is high in achievement motivation from the person who is low in achievement motivation. The study of self-confidence has a more cognitive flavour and addresses the individual's confidence in particular situations and their perception of their own ability, rather than taking a general view of self-confidence as a personality trait.

SELF-EFFICACY – BANDURA

Bandura (1977b) proposed that as people learn that they can master things they develop a feeling of **self-efficacy**, the expectation that they will be competent and successful in a particular task. Bandura (1982) found that those with high levels of self-efficacy try harder and persist longer, whereas those low in self-efficacy give up in the face of difficulty, attribute failure to internal causes (they blame themselves), and experience greater anxiety or depression.

Bandura suggests that expectations of efficacy are the major reasons for our choice of activity, the amount of effort we put into it and the degree of persistence we show: in other words, expectations of efficacy explain motivation. He proposed that self-efficacy comes from four sources:

1. **Successful performance** – previous experiences provide information from which self-efficacy develops. Past success increases self-efficacy, indeed this is the most important influence on self-efficacy. Once self-efficacy is established the individual is better able to tolerate some failure.
2. **Vicarious experiences** – this means watching others successfully perform the task. After observing successful models, the individual

usually approaches his or her own efforts with more confidence.
3. **Verbal persuasion** – encouraging the performer to think they can do the task. A team-mate who says 'Come on, you can do it' may increase her partner's self-efficacy (although persuasion does not appear to be a very powerful influence on self-efficacy).
4. **Arousal** – the way the performer interprets the arousal they feel will affect their feelings of confidence. Research with swimmers, cricketers and gymnasts suggests that positive perceptions of arousal are related to higher levels of confidence.

Bandura proposed that these four sources of self-efficacy combine to increase expectations of success, which in turn affects performance. Self-efficacy is dynamic. It will vary due to these four factors and how they interact together. Thus, self-efficacy is the mediating variable – the link between these four sources and athletic performance. Figure 3.2 below shows this relationship in diagram form.

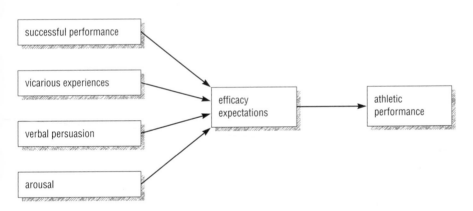

• **Figure 3.2:** The relationship between self-efficacy, four sources of information and performance

SPORT-SPECIFIC MODEL OF SPORT CONFIDENCE – VEALEY

Vealey (1986) views sport confidence as the degree of certainty that a person has about their ability to be successful in sport. She has devised a model of sport confidence which includes both the athlete's personality trait of sport confidence (**SC-trait**), and the athlete's **competitive orientation**, which is their approach to competition (and is related to Gill and Deeter's SOQ). These two combine to predict the athlete's confidence in a particular sporting situation, which is called state sport confidence (**SC-state**). This in turn predicts the athlete's performance, possible outcomes and the athlete's interpretation of outcomes. These affect the two determinants of sport confidence – the personality trait of sport confidence and the competitive orientation. Figure 3.3 illustrates the relationships between the elements in Vealey's model.

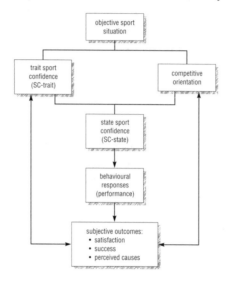

• **Figure 3.3:** Vealey's model of sport confidence (based on Cox, 1994, p.225)

Cox (1998) considers the approach valuable because it enables predictions to be made about an athlete's confidence in a specific sport situation, as well as explaining how sport confidence develops from sport experiences. He comments that Vealey's model has been generated from within the sport experience, rather than being adapted from theories within general psychology. In order to test the model, Vealey devised measures of SC-trait, SC-state and competitive orientation. She reports that the model is supported by her research using these measures.

Section summary   This section has looked at Bandura's theory of self-efficacy and Vealey's model of sport confidence, both of which consider confidence in one's own ability to be ever-changing and due in part to past experiences. Bandura's model includes awareness of arousal and the role of others in the development of self-efficacy. By contrast, Vealey's model is focused on the individual's beliefs and perceptions about their ability to be successful in sport.

Improving motivation and self-confidence

In this final section we identify ways of improving motivation and self-confidence in a sport setting, using principles from several psychological theories.

EXTRINSIC AND INTRINSIC MOTIVATION

According to the principles of **learning theory**, behaviour is more likely to be repeated if it is rewarded. The reward acts as **reinforcement** which motivates the behaviour (for more details see Theme link, p.26). Motivation may depend on external rewards (**extrinsic motivation**) or internal rewards (**intrinsic motivation**). As you will see below, these two types of motivation have a different effect on the individual's attitude and success in physical activities.

intrinsic motivation

The 40-year-old who takes up marathon running, training three nights a week and on Sundays, is more likely to be motivated by intrinsic rewards, such as the satisfaction of an improved finishing time, than by the winner's medal. Deci (1975) proposed that behaviours which are intrinsically motivating are 'those which a person engages in to feel competent and self-determining' (p.61).

Intrinsic motivation arises spontaneously. It does not have to be provided by others. It is also persistent. We continue to seek out opportunities to feel 'competent and self-determining'.

extrinsic motivation

By its very nature sport provides many examples of extrinsic motivation. These include tangible rewards, such as trophies or medals.

• **Figure 3.4:** Trophies provide extrinsic motivation: Venus Williams (US) celebrates after defeating Lindsay Davenport to win her first Wimbledon Ladies Single title

Sport also provides less tangible reinforcements, such as prestige or praise. These are known as **social reinforcements**. Smith, Smoll and Curtis (1979) reported that children who were given encouragement by their coaches reported greater enjoyment and enthusiasm for the coming season than children who were not. In addition, this positive approach had the most dramatic impact on children who started with the lowest levels of self-esteem.

As a result of their research on sports coaching for young people, Smith and Smoll (1984) produced guidelines for coaches' behaviour. They recommended that extrinsic rewards should be:

- given as a result of a particular behaviour rather than a generalised 'well done' – for example, providing feedback about correct footwork.
- given as soon as possible after the behaviour occurs – so that the association between the behaviour (correct footwork) and the reinforcement ('nice footwork there!') is strengthened.
- applied intermittently – so that the behaviour continues even when reinforcement does not follow (see partial reinforcement, p.26).

the relationship between extrinsic and intrinsic motivation

Extrinsic rewards can make the individual more likely to perform the behaviours which are being rewarded. For this reason, it might be assumed

• **Figure 3.5:** According to Lepper & Greene's research, this youngster's pleasure may be reduced if he is given a reward for playing

that levels of motivation will increase if we give an extrinsic reward (such as a trophy) to someone who is already intrinsically motivated. However, it seems that extrinsic motivation may damage intrinsic motivation and lead to a decrease in performance, as described by Lepper and Greene (1975).

When they observed a group of children who were drawing, they noted that the children who had been rewarded subsequently spent less time drawing than those who had not been rewarded.

In his **cognitive evaluation theory**, Deci (1975) proposed that it is the person's interpretation of the reward, not the reward itself, which affects intrinsic motivation. If the reward is seen as controlling the behaviour ('I am doing this to get praise from my coach') the athlete's sense of self-determination is low, and therefore intrinsic motivation is damaged. In contrast, if the reward enhances feelings of self-competence then intrinsic motivation is increased ('The coach said my footwork was good, so I can get it right'). In research with cricketers, Woodcock and Corbin (1992) found that intrinsic motivation was strengthened by positive feedback after they had successfully mastered new skills.

GOAL-SETTING

Most of us are good at setting goals – New Year's resolutions, losing weight, saving up – but poor at achieving them. However goal-setting has been found to lead to improved performance in many workplace settings, evidence explained by Locke and Latham's (1990) **goal-setting theory**. This is a cognitive theory of motivation which proposes that goals which are difficult and specific should lead to higher levels of performance.

According to Locke et al. (1981), goal-setting can influence performance because it: directs attention to the task; mobilises effort (making the individual work harder); increases persistence (enabling the individual to achieve long-term goals); helps the development of new learning strategies.

As a result of research into the theory, several principles have been devised which are likely to contribute to improved performance. These are that goals should be:

- **Specific** – rather than just being told to 'try harder', identifying specific goals tells the athlete exactly what he is working towards, and when it has been achieved.
- **Controllable** – goals should be within the athlete's control. He should therefore be encouraged to set performance goals (aimed at improving his own skills), rather than outcome goals over which he has less control. Outcome goals depend on the performance of others – for example, winning a race depends on the quality of fellow competitors, or winning a football match depends on team-mates. This is substantiated by Burton's (1989) research with swimmers, in a paper entitled 'Winning isn't everything'.

- **Challenging** – because a challenging goal provides satisfaction (intrinsic motivation) when it is achieved. The needs and abilities of the athlete are crucial in determining what is challenging. For example, athletes with a high motive to avoid failure may set inappropriate goals which ensure either success or failure.
- **Attainable** – goals must be realistic and therefore attainable, because it is the achievement of the goal which increases performance and motivation. This is a controversial aspect of Locke and Latham's theory, which predicted that the more difficult the goal, the better the performance. However, subsequent research such as that by Kyllo and Landers (1995) concludes that moderate goals are more effective than difficult ones. Long-term goals will be more attainable if they are broken down into short-term goals.
- **Measurable** – devising goals which can be easily measured and recorded, such as performance time, gives the athlete accessible and explicit feedback.
- **Personal** – which means goals should relate to the individual's own needs, ability, attitude, anxiety level, self-confidence and so on. Goals should be decided jointly by athlete and coach/teacher, so that the athlete feels committed to achieving the goal.

Interestingly, although research into goal-setting shows that it is valuable in the workplace, results in sports-based research are less conclusive. For example, when participants in an experimental group have been given specific goals to achieve, and a control group has been told to 'do your best', the improvements in the two groups have often been at similar levels. Weinberg, Bruya and Jackson (1985) gave a follow-up questionnaire to the 'do your best' participants, finding many who said they had set their own targets. It may be that sportspeople, whether in training or in competition, are more likely to set themselves specific targets than non-sports participants. Nevertheless, the principles we have reviewed above will help coaches and performers set more effective goals.

IMPROVING SELF-EFFICACY

Using Bandura's model, efficacy expectations can be improved by tackling any of the four sources of self-efficacy. For example:

- **Successful performance** – players should be given opportunities to experience success, particularly those new to the sport. Athletes should be encouraged to take pride and satisfaction in past successes, and to judge these in terms of personal performance (have a performance orientation) rather than outcome (the win orientation). Failures should be seen positively (as opportunities to learn) and dealt with quickly so that the athlete's attention is focused on the next goal.

- **Vicarious experiences** – the sportsperson should have opportunities to watch others be successful, particularly against difficult opponents or when the model has gone through a bad patch and yet pulled themselves around. Gould and Weiss (1981) reported that self-efficacy was improved by watching similar models.
- **Verbal persuasion** – we noted that this does not appear to have a significant effect on self-efficacy, but if it is appropriate and well-timed it may provide a boost to self-efficacy.
- **Arousal** – if the sportsperson can see arousal as positive, this will help them feel prepared physically and mentally. For more on arousal and anxiety, see Chapter 4.

The sports performer's attributions (see p.68) are also linked to self-efficacy. Jourden, Bandura and Banfield (1991) reported that athletes who believed that their performance at an activity was due to innate ability (an **internal stable attribution**) showed little interest in developing the skill. It appears that self-efficacy develops when the athlete believes it is their own efforts (an **internal unstable attribution**) which lead to improved performance. Bandura acknowledged that factors such as having the necessary skills, setting appropriate goals, making the correct attributions and feeling mentally and physically ready will also affect performance.

IMPROVING MOTIVATION IN CHILDREN

Many of the techniques in this section can be used with children. But psychologists who view achievement from a developmental perspective have highlighted the way in which the child's needs and abilities change as they grow up. If motivation in children is to be improved, teachers and coaches must keep these developmental changes in mind.

Theme link to Perspectives **(the developmental approach)**

Developmental psychologists study how children's behaviour and thinking change as they mature. One change is in their understanding of themselves in relation to others. As children get older their understanding becomes more complex and more abstract. The young child tends to see herself as the centre of her world, but as she gets older she takes more account of other people, their understanding and abilities. The older child is also able to understand more abstract concepts such as the rules of games. These changes are described in **Piaget's theory of cognitive development** and are applicable to many aspects of the child's development.

Veroff (1969) has proposed three stages in the development of achievement motivation which reflect the changes summarised in the Theme Link box. The stages are described below along with suggestions for improving motivation in children.

autonomous competence stage

Up to about five years of age the child is most concerned with mastering skills, so she will repeat the same actions such as jumping off the stairs. She is not interested in whether someone else can jump further. Her concern is to do better than she did last time – she has a performance orientation, setting her own goals and experiencing intrinsic motivation. There is little point in setting up competitive situations for the under-fives, but their fascination with mastery can be put to good use in helping them develop basic skills such as balancing, throwing, catching and running.

social comparison stage

By about six years the child starts to compare herself with others – who is the tallest, fastest, strongest – she is developing a win, or outcome, orientation. Children tend to use competition mainly to beat others and to satisfy their own egos, so to counteract this they can be helped to focus on setting their own targets for their own improvements – to become goal (or performance) oriented. A Canadian sport psychologist argues that there is too much competition in children's sport (Orlick 1978). He has developed games which encourage fun, allow freedom to make mistakes and be sensitive to others' feelings.

One of Orlick's concerns is the child who is uncomfortable in competitive situations or always performs poorly. This child may withdraw from sports activity unless she has sensitive support. This support could include providing some reinforcement, encouraging self-confidence, increasing the social/fun element of her participation or perhaps finding a sport more suited to her abilities.

integrated stage

Appropriate support at the previous stage will help the child achieve the final stage. This is not associated with a specific age, but depends on the child's maturation, her experiences and her understanding of them. This final stage is reached when she uses both outcome and performance orientation, and knows when it is appropriate to use each one.

Section summary   This section has described several ways of improving motivation and self-confidence, whilst warning against some of the damaging effects they may have. The techniques, used appropriately, may help motivate performers of all ages and abilities.

KEY TERMS

achievement motivation
autonomous competence stage
cognitive evaluation theory
competitiveness
competitive orientation
developmental approach
extrinsic motivation
goal orientation
goal-setting
incentive value of success
integrated stage
internal stable attribution
internal unstable attribution
intrinsic motivation
learning theory
motive to achieve success
motive to avoid failure
outcome orientation
performance orientation
Piaget's theory of cognitive
   development
reinforcement
SC-state
SC-trait
self-efficacy
social comparison stage
social reinforcement
sport-specific achievement
   motivation
task difficulty
task orientation
win orientation

EXERCISE **1**

Explain the difference between outcome orientation and
performance orientation, giving an example of each from a sport of
your choice.

EXERCISE **2**

Devise an example of intrinsic motivation, and an example of extrinsic motivation which might damage it. Do this for an 11-year-old and for an adult. Compare your answers with a partner.

EXERCISE **3**

Give three examples of the way self-efficacy can affect a sportsperson's behaviour.

ESSAY QUESTIONS

1. Describe a model of achievement motivation.

2. Discuss the reasons why a sport-specific model of self-confidence may be a better predictor of performance than a general model of self-confidence.

3. You are a tennis coach who is devising an introductory programme for adult beginners. Explain how you would use your knowledge of self-efficacy to devise this programme.

Further reading

Bakker, F. C., Whiting, H. T. A. and van der Brug, H. (1990) *Sport Psychology: Concepts and Applications*. Chichester: John Wiley & Sons (Chapter 2).

Cox, R. H. (1998) *Sport Psychology: Concepts and Applications* (4th ed.). Boston, MA: WCB McGraw-Hill (Chapter 8).

Gill, D. L. (1986) *Psychological Dynamics of Sport*. Champaign, IL: Human Kinetics Publishers (Chapters 5 and 10).

Hardy, L., Jones, G. and Gould, D. (1996) *Understanding Psychological Preparation for Sport*. Chichester: John Wiley & Sons. (Chapters 3 and 4).

Horn, T. S. (Ed) (1992) *Advances in Sport Psychology*. Champaign, IL: Human Kinetics Publishers (Chapter 4 and 5).

Morris, T. and Summers, J. (Eds) (1995) *Sport Psychology – Theory, Applications and Issues.* Milton, Queensland: John Wiley & Sons (Chapters 4, 6, 10 and 13).

Pargman, D. (1998) *Understanding Sport Behaviour.* Upper Saddle River, NJ: Prentice Hall, Inc. (Chapter 4).

Wann, D. L. (1997) *Sport Psychology.* Upper Saddle River, NJ: Prentice Hall, Inc. (Chapter 8).

Websites

http://www.mindtools.com/selfconf.html – benefits of self-confidence to sports-people and how to develop it.

http://www.mindtools.com/goalsett.html – advice and application of goal setting to sport situation.

http://www.emory.edu/EDUCATION/mfp/aera1.html – details of Bandura's work on self-efficacy, its application and future research.

4
Arousal and anxiety in sport

The pressure of competition can pep up an athlete's performance or damage it. Most sportspeople associate competition with feeling alert and ready, yet they may also experience apprehension, sweaty palms or fear about their performance. If we can find out why this happens, we can help performers reduce these effects so as to improve their performance.

IN THIS CHAPTER WE WILL EXAMINE:

- theories of arousal
- types and measures of anxiety
- reducing anxiety and optimising arousal.

Theories of arousal

Arousal is a **physiological** state of alertness and anticipation which prepares the body for action. We need the appropriate level of activation for the action we are to perform (known as optimal arousal), whether it is digesting a meal or catching a cricket ball. We will now consider two theories which explain the relationship between arousal and performance: drive theory and the inverted U hypothesis. These early theories of arousal come from mainstream psychology rather than sport psychology.

DRIVE THEORY

Drive theory was developed by Hull (1951) and Spence (1956) and its key component is the performer's level of skill. **Drive theory** predicts that drive, which is essentially the same as **arousal**, strengthens the performance of the **dominant response**. In other words, if a skill is well-learned then it will be performed even better with increased arousal. However, if the skill is not well-learned then the dominant response will be incorrect, so as arousal increases, performance of the skill will deteriorate.

Clearly the impact of arousal on performance is complex. Consider these two accounts of arousal and performance from Hemery (1986).

Case study   Ed Moses, Olympic medal winner in the 1976 and 1984 400m hurdles, said 'the way I get the best out is by not expecting an easy race. It's easier when there's pressure. You get emotional and go out to perform' (p.163).

Bob Tisdall described a fellow student at Cambridge who desperately wanted to win a race for the University in order to get a 'blue'. He stayed on for a fourth year especially to have another chance. Tisdall reported that the student 'froze in the starting blocks in the finals. We had to pick him up and he was stiff, like a corpse' (p.131).

Arousal improved Ed Moses' performance but devastated the performance of the Cambridge student. Both athletes were performing well-learned tasks. Drive theory fails to explain this outcome, and its focus on the well-learned task cannot be applied to the many sports skills which combine both well-learned and novel elements.

INVERTED U HYPOTHESIS

The **inverted U hypothesis** accounts for some of the criticisms of drive theory and states that arousal causes an improvement in performance, but only up to a point – called the **optimal point**. As arousal increases beyond that point, performance deteriorates. When this is plotted on a graph, it is shaped like an inverted 'U', as shown in Figure 4.1. You can see that performance is at its optimal when there is a moderate level of arousal. Research has shown that this inverted U relationship exists in a number of different circumstances, such as:

- **Type of skill** – Oxendine (1970) proposed that the amount of arousal necessary for optimal performance depended on the nature of the skill. As an example, optimal performance when putting in golf requires a low level of arousal (high arousal interferes with fine muscle movement co-ordination and concentration) whereas tackling in football requires a high level of arousal (which helps skills requiring speed or strength) as shown in Figure 4.1. Critics argue that many skills involve both strength and complexity, which are difficult to separate out.

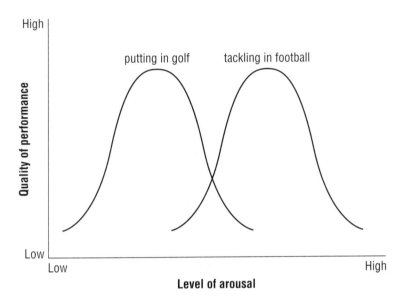

High

Quality of performance

putting in golf   tackling in football

Low

Low   High

Level of arousal

• **Figure 4.1:** The relationship between level of arousal and optimal level of performance in golf and football

- **Nature of environment** – skills which are performed in an unpredictable environment make more cognitive demands on the performer. A high level of arousal will damage the performance of a netball player: she must perform complex motor skills whilst simultaneously judging the flight of the ball, monitoring the movement of team-mates and the opposition and making decisions about tactics. In contrast, a weightlifter performs in a predictable environment which makes few cognitive demands.

- **Level of expertise** – a beginner needs only very low levels of arousal to perform well. Because control of the skill is not yet automatic, the learner uses his cognitive abilities to direct, monitor and control the skill (for further details see Attentional capacity, p.113). In contrast, such low levels of arousal will have no effect on the elite performer, who needs much higher levels to produce optimal performance. The inverted U relationship between arousal and level of expertise is shown in Figure 4.2.

TYPES OF AROUSAL

So far we have looked at the relationship between arousal and performance, but we have not yet considered arousal itself. You will see from the three types of arousal noted by Lacey (1967) why arousal may have the differing effects that were noted under the inverted U hypothesis.

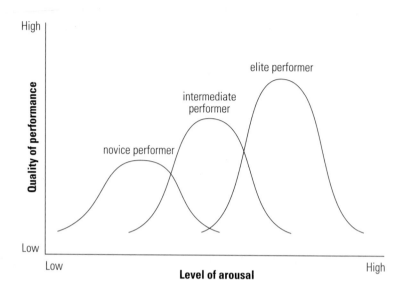

• **Figure 4.2:** The relationship between level of arousal and level of expertise

electrocortical arousal

This is arousal of the brain. It refers to increased electrical activity in the cortex, which is measured by an electroencephalogram (EEG). This activity may lead to confused thinking and changes in attention and concentration which can damage performance (see Attention, p.113).

autonomic arousal

This refers to increased activity in the autonomic nervous system. This activity can be measured by noting physiological changes in:

* heart rate, which is measured using an electrocardiogram (ECG) or by measuring the pulse
* breathing rate
* muscle tension, which is measured using an electromyogram (EMG)
* sweating on the palm of the hand, which can be measured using the galvanic skin response (GSR) by attaching electrodes to the palms of the hand and connecting them to a voltage meter
* the level of hormones and steroids in the blood or urine.

Lacey (1967) noted that it was possible for activity in one system to be high whilst in another system it was low, and that different tasks triggered different patterns of activity. For example, in behaviour involving reaction time (such as saving a penalty in soccer) heart rate is lowered but skin conductance is usually raised. When stressful cognitive activity is involved, such as deciding how to play a difficult shot at golf, both of these are usually lowered.

In addition, individuals vary in their physiological responses, so that one person may show a rapid increase in heart and breathing rate whereas another may show only an increase in galvanic skin response.

behavioural changes

Arousal may cause behavioural changes such as particular facial expressions, changes in patterns of speech, negative self-talk, fidgeting, licking the lips, rubbing the palms of the hands on clothing, restless pacing, trembling hands. Changes in performance of skills may also occur, such as level of accuracy or speed of reaction.

> **Section summary**
>
> In this section we have seen that drive theory, which predicts a linear relationship between arousal and performance, does not reflect performance as accurately as the inverted U hypothesis. The inverted U relationship has been found in many sports situations, reflecting factors such as skill level and type of skill, and understanding the different types of arousal helps to explain some of these variations.

Types and measures of anxiety

Although arousal is a neutral physiological state, **anxiety** is the negative emotional state associated with arousal. Anxiety can be defined as the feelings of apprehension and awareness of heightened arousal which are often associated with fears, worries and doubts. Anxiety may be caused by situations which are seen as threatening because we doubt our ability to cope with them, for example situations which:

*   threaten our self-esteem – such as being embarrassed
*   cause personal harm – for example when going into a rough game
*   create uncertainty or fear of the unknown – as when a player is waiting to hear whether she has been selected
*   create frustration – such as being unable to achieve our goals
*   create pressure – for example taking the penalty shot to win the match.

A variety of pencil and paper tests have been devised to measure various types of anxiety. Details are given in this section as the different types of anxiety are described. As anxiety has a physiological component, physiological measures can also be used. Details of physiological changes, and how they are measured, have been described on p.54, and some of the problems are noted in the Theme Link box below.

Theme link to Methodology **(evaluation of methods)**

The use of physiological methods poses some problems in research. For example, it is cumbersome to 'wire up' the athlete in order to take these measures, which need to be taken before, during and after activity if they are to be of use. Being wired up may increase the athlete's level of arousal because it interferes with their ability to perform and also affects their awareness of their performance. Therefore, the measuring of arousal itself may cause increased arousal, thus making results less valid. Athletes may be reluctant to be tested in a competitive setting and risk jeopardising their performance in the name of psychological research. The alternative is a laboratory setting, which is artifical and may not be an accurate reproduction of the competitive situation.

Some people seem to be anxious most of the time about something, others do not, and this is reflected in Spielberger's (1971) distinction between trait anxiety and state anxiety.

TRAIT ANXIETY

This refers to a predisposition to see situations as threatening. Someone who easily becomes anxious, even about non-threatening situations, has high **trait anxiety,** which is seen as a personality trait. Researchers have devised methods of measuring trait anxiety, such as Martens' (1977) Sport Competition Anxiety Test (SCAT). This pencil and paper test asks the performer specific questions relating to their feelings in a pre-competitive situation. Responses are scored to give a level of competitive trait anxiety.

STATE ANXIETY

State anxiety refers to a temporary emotional state which involves feelings of apprehension and fear along with physiological arousal. Spielberger predicts that individuals with high trait anxiety will perceive more situations as threatening, and respond to challenges with more state anxiety than individuals with low trait anxiety.

A further distinction which has been found useful is that between the mental and physical effects of anxiety. These are known as:

- **somatic state anxiety** – perception of bodily symptoms of anxiety, such as sweating palms, butterflies; this perception is directly linked to arousal.
- **cognitive state anxiety** – worry, negative thoughts about performance, fear of failure, loss of self-esteem, disrupted attention, inability to concentrate.

The next section describes more recent models of anxiety and illustrates the benefits of separating out these two types of anxiety. These models relate to performance, and therefore to state anxiety, so the word 'state' is often excluded because it is taken for granted.

THE MULTIDIMENSIONAL MODEL OF ANXIETY

A study of swimmers conducted by Burton (1988) showed that somatic state anxiety had the predicted relationship to performance – optimal performance occurred when somatic state anxiety was at a moderate level. However, when the level of cognitive state anxiety was measured, Burton found the lower the cognitive anxiety the better the performance. A graph showing these results is given in Figure 4.3.

This graph shows an inverted U relationship between somatic anxiety and performance, but a negative linear relationship between cognitive anxiety and performance. In other words, the greater the cognitive anxiety the worse the

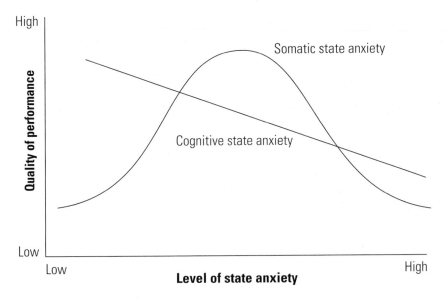

• **Figure 4.3:** The relationship between performance, cognitive and somatic state anxiety

Competitive State Anxiety Inventory-2 (CSAI-2)

Directions: a number of statements which athletes have used to describe their feelings before competition are given below. Read each statement and then circle the appropriate number to the right of the statement to indicate how you feel right now – at this moment. There are no right or wrong answers. Do not spend too much time on any one statement, but choose the answer which describes your feelings right now.

	Not at all	Somewhat	Moderately so	Very much so
1 I am concerned about this competition	1	2	3	4
2 I feel nervous	1	2	3	4
3 I feel at ease	1	2	3	4
4 I have self-doubts	1	2	3	4
5 I feel jittery	1	2	3	4
6 I feel comfortable	1	2	3	4
7 I am concerned that I may not do so well in this competition as I could	1	2	3	4
8 My body feels tense	1	2	3	4
9 I feel self-confident	1	2	3	4
10 I am concerned about losing	1	2	3	4
11 I feel tense in my stomach	1	2	3	4
12 I feel secure	1	2	3	4
13 I am concerned about choking under pressure	1	2	3	4
14 My body feels relaxed	1	2	3	4
15 I'm confident I can meet the challenge	1	2	3	4
16 I'm concerned about performing poorly	1	2	3	4
17 My heart is racing	1	2	3	4
18 I'm confident about performing well	1	2	3	4
19 I'm concerned about reaching my goal	1	2	3	4
20 I feel my stomach sinking	1	2	3	4
21 I feel mentally relaxed	1	2	3	4
22 I'm concerned that others will be disappointed with my performance	1	2	3	4
23 My hands are clammy	1	2	3	4
24 I'm confident because I mentally picture myself reaching my goal	1	2	3	4
25 I'm concerned I won't be able to concentrate	1	2	3	4
26 My body feels tight	1	2	3	4
27 I'm confident of coming through under pressure	1	2	3	4

• **Figure 4.4:** An extract from the CSAI-2 questionnaire

performance. Because of results such as these, Martens, Vealey and Burton (1990) argued for a **multidimensional** view of anxiety. They propose that in a competitive situation anxiety has three components:

- cognitive state anxiety
- somatic state anxiety
- self-confidence – expectations of success or failure.

They developed the Competitive State Anxiety Inventory (**CSAI-2**, see Figure 4.4) which is a self-report questionnaire measuring each of these three components. Questions relate to the participant's somatic anxiety level (q.8), their cognitive anxiety level (q.22), and their self-confidence (q.27).

Athletes are asked how they feel at various times, so questionnaires are carried out one week before a major competition, then again 24 hours before, then again 30 minutes before. This enables the researchers to establish a 'baseline' level of anxiety and the level of anxiety immediately before competition. The difference between the two gives the measure of state anxiety. In addition they can establish which types of anxiety are more evident at which point in the pre-competition period.

Using the CSAI-2, and several other inventories which measure the multidimensional nature of anxiety, researchers have found two different patterns, one for cognitive and one for somatic anxiety:

- **Cognitive anxiety** increases during the days before competition, remains high but does not increase just before competition starts. Once performance is under way cognitive anxiety fluctuates, usually as the likelihood of success or failure changes. Research suggests that high cognitive state anxiety has a major impact on performance. Bird and Horn (1990) found for example that mental errors made in women's softball were directly related to high cognitive state anxiety.
- **Somatic anxiety** tends to be low but rises quickly a few hours before the event and decreases during competition. The difference between these two patterns of anxiety is shown in Figure 4.5.

CATASTROPHE THEORY

Two British sport psychologists (Fazey and Hardy, 1988) note that performance does not always gradually deteriorate as arousal increases, as shown in the inverted U hypothesis. Instead there is sometimes a dramatic decline – a **catastrophe** in performance. How can both of these outcomes be explained? Fazey and Hardy argue that somatic and cognitive anxiety do not just have a different effect on performance (see Figure 4.3) but that they interact: they have an effect on each other. Fazey and Hardy propose that:

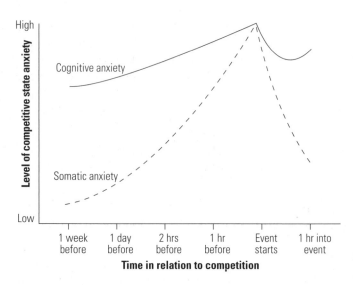

• **Figure 4.5:** Changes in cognitive and somatic anxiety in the pre-competition period

- increases in cognitive anxiety will have a beneficial effect on performance if the performer is at a low level of somatic anxiety (physiological arousal)
- increases in cognitive anxiety will have a detrimental effect on performance at high levels of physiological arousal
- if cognitive anxiety is high then continuing increases in physiological arousal can cause a large and sudden deterioration in performance – the catastrophe
- if a catastrophe does occur, small reductions in arousal will not bring performance back to its previous level. Instead the performer must relax in order to bring arousal below the point where the catastrophe occurred.

Essentially Fazey and Hardy contend that physiological arousal has a 'normal' impact but cognitive anxiety has a 'splitting' effect – it is cognitive anxiety which determines whether changes in performance are gradual or dramatic. This explains the results of research such as that by Bird and Horn (p.59), which found that high cognitive anxiety has a major impact on performance.

Section summary   The inter-relationship between arousal and anxiety has been explored in this section, as we examined different types of anxiety and their effects on sport performance. The differences between the physical and mental effects of state anxiety have been incorporated in the multi-dimensional model of the relationship between anxiety and performance. Catastrophe theory proposes that not only do these two operate differently, but that they have an interactive effect on performance.

Reducing anxiety and optimising arousal

Arousal is not only a feature of the competitive situation, but of several other situations covered in this book, such as the effect of an audience and Eysenck's introversion–extroversion dimension of personality. The techniques described in this section can be used in ways which correspond to the individual's needs. These will depend on factors such as the individual's patterns of arousal and their sport situation at that time.

The techniques can be classed as mainly somatic (relating to the body) or cognitive (relating to thinking). However, as we have seen, sportspeople may experience both kinds of anxiety at the same time and the relationship between arousal and anxiety is complex. As a result, although a technique may be classed as somatic it will probably also have cognitive elements.

SOMATIC TECHNIQUES

The purpose behind somatic techniques is to reduce the physiological responses associated with arousal.

biofeedback

In **biofeedback** the athlete uses physiological measuring equipment to help him learn how to control his physiological responses. For example, when the athlete can hear his heartbeat he can try to think of something calming, to find out which thoughts lead to a slowing down of the heart rate. With practice he will be able to use these thoughts in order to decrease heart rate and arousal.

Some of the other measures which can be used are:

- thermometer attached to a finger – because high arousal causes less blood to go to the fingers, they become cold. The athlete watches the thermometer as he tries to control his responses.
- electromyogram to measure muscular tension – the measures taken by the electromyogram can be shown on a meter which makes a loud sound when muscle tension is high. The athlete tries to reduce the sound level by reducing muscle tension. This can be done using some of the techniques examined below.

breathing

Increase in breathing rate is a result of increased arousal, so reducing the breathing rate is one of the easiest ways to bring arousal under control. Muscle tension is released by breathing out, so athletes need first to take deep breaths but they also need to breathe out at the appropriate time in their performance. For example, a gymnast should take a deep breath and let the air out slowly and thoroughly immediately before starting her routine. Taking in and holding the breath causes muscle tension and is therefore damaging to performance.

There are additional advantages to using breathing control. Not only does it reduce arousal level and muscle tension, but it also helps focus, so that irrelevant cues are less likely to create distraction. It is also a very quick and simple technique, so it can be used in all sports situations, whether training, injury rehabilitation or competition. Finally, it provides a brief break from the pressure of the situation, so it helps performers gather their thoughts and energies. The value of breathing control is endorsed by Mary Nevill, as you will see in the next section.

relaxation

Somatic anxiety causes muscle tension, but because it is not possible to be relaxed and tense at the same time, the development of relaxation techniques can reduce tension. One widely used method of physical relaxation is **progressive muscular relaxation** (PMR). This involves tensing and then relaxing groups of muscles in turn over the whole body. Athletes often devise their own techniques along these lines, and practice usually enables the athlete to relax effectively in a very short period of time. Mary Nevill, captain of the British hockey team in the 1992 Olympics, reports that she relaxes her shoulders by just dropping them and taking a deep breath (Jones and Hardy, 1990).

Other types of relaxation, such as meditation or hypnotism, involve both physical and mental aspects. Meditation usually involves breathing control and techniques to help clear the mind of other thoughts, such as focusing attention on a word or sound, or perhaps repeating a special word (known as a mantra). This should take place in a quiet environment.

Hypnosis is not used frequently, and because its effects are not fully understood it should only be practised by trained professionals. Once hypnotised and in a relaxed state the individual is given suggestions such as 'when you prepare to receive serve you will feel relaxed and confident'. You can see that these suggestions are aimed at reducing both somatic and cognitive anxiety.

COGNITIVE TECHNIQUES

Cognitive techniques emphasise the role of thought processes in managing anxiety and arousal. A brief summary is given below.

imagery

Imagery is often used with the relaxation techniques we noted above in order to reduce arousal. The athlete imagines the circumstances and feelings associated with being relaxed, for example imagining floating in warm water. For more on imagery see p.119.

self-talk

Rather than interpret arousal as damaging performance, the athlete can see it as positive, saying 'I'm ready for this'. Self-talk can be used to put the situation in a different perspective and make it seem less threatening. A tennis player who is becoming very anxious in a match could say: 'What is the absolutely worst thing that can happen? – I can lose a tennis match'. For more on self-talk see 'reducing aggression' on p.31.

cognitive relabelling

When about to perform, the athlete may label her arousal as apprehension, which is negative. Alternatively she may label it as excitement, which is positive and should contribute to a good performance. For this reason, changing the athlete's cognitive appraisal of the situation may lead to a change in emotion, according to Kagan (1975).

Schachter and Singer (1962) created arousal in their participants, some of whom were told to expect feelings of arousal. However, the other participants labelled their arousal in accordance with the context they were in. Those who were with someone who seemed happy reported happiness, those with an angry person reported feeling anger. Schachter and Singer concluded that an individual who is in a state of physiological arousal and has no clear explanation for it will label his arousal in accordance with his understanding of his environment.

Schachter and Singer proposed that both physiological arousal and cognitive interpretation are necessary for an emotional experience. The label we attach to our arousal depends on what we attribute the arousal to, which is why it is called 'cognitive labelling theory'.

Core Study – Cognitive, social and physiological determinants of emotional state.

Interpretation of arousal can change very rapidly in a sports setting. Envisage the rugby player kicking a conversion to take the lead. He will label his arousal before the kick as apprehension, but this will change immediately if he is successful, when he might label the arousal as joy or exhilaration.

self-confidence

Self-confidence helps protect the sportsperson from the effects of arousal, as we saw in the discussion of self-efficacy (p.45). Certainly the vast majority of elite performers cite **self-confidence** as a major feature of their success. It helps them see arousal as positive rather than negative. For example, research with swimmers, cricketers and gymnasts suggest that higher levels of confidence are related to positive perceptions of arousal. Increasing the performer's self-confidence should therefore reduce the negative effects of arousal.

Section summary   This section has discussed some of the techniques for reducing anxiety and optimising arousal in competitive situations. These techniques have both somatic and cognitive elements, and may be used in combination to strengthen their effect. Earlier in the chapter we considered individual differences in anxiety. Clearly the needs of the performer and other factors, such as their skill level and the type of sport, will determine which of the above techniques will be of greatest value.

KEY TERMS

anxiety
arousal
autonomic arousal
biofeedback
catastrophe theory
cognitive relabelling
cognitive state anxiety
competitive state anxiety
CSAI-2
dominant response
drive theory
electrocortical arousal
imagery
inverted U hypothesis
multidimensional model
optimal point
physiological
progressive muscular relaxation
SCAT
self-confidence
self-talk
somatic state anxiety
state anxiety
trait anxiety

EXERCISE **1**

Using examples from sport, explain the difference between trait anxiety and state anxiety.

EXERCISE **2**

Give two examples of the impact which electrocortical arousal can have on thought processes. The material in Chapter 8 may help.

EXERCISE **3**

Working in small groups, devise an observation schedule for recording behavioural changes in a professional footballer during the 30 minutes before kick-off.

ESSAY QUESTIONS

1. Describe the inverted U hypothesis as it relates to a sport performer.

2. Using your knowledge of various types of anxiety, how would you explain why a student 'froze in the starting blocks'?

3. Identify two reasons why self-confidence might protect the sportsperson from the negative effects of arousal. Explain why each of them might have this effect.

Further reading

Cox, R. H. (1998) *Sport Psychology: Concepts and Applications* (4th ed.). Boston, MA: WCB McGraw-Hill (Chapter 4).

Gill, D. L. (1986) *Psychological Dynamics of Sport*. Champaign, IL: Human Kinetics Publishers (Chapter 8).

Hardy, L., Jones, G. and Gould, D. (1996) *Understanding Psychological Preparation for Sport*. Chichester: John Wiley & Sons. (Chapters 5 and 6).

Horn, T. S. (Ed) (1992) *Advances in Sport Psychology*. Champaign, IL: Human Kinetics Publishers (Chapter 6).

Kremer, J. and Scully, D. (1994) *Psychology in Sport.* London: Taylor & Francis (Chapter 4).

Morris, T. and Summers, J. (Eds) (1995) *Sport Psychology – Theory, Applications and Issues*. Milton, Queensland: John Wiley & Sons (Chapters 5 and 11).

Pargman, D. (1998) *Understanding Sport Behaviour.* Upper Saddle River, NJ: Prentice Hall, Inc. (Chapter 2).

Wann, D. L. (1997) *Sport Psychology*. Upper Saddle River, NJ: Prentice Hall, Inc. (Chapters 7 and 10).

Websites

http://www.mindtools.com/stresscn.html – provides background and links to techniques for reduction of stress.

http://www.geocities.com/CollegePark/5686/su99p16.htm – the report of a study into state and trait anxiety in two basketball situations, using CSAI-2 and SCAT.

http://www.brianmac.demon.co.uk – some relaxation techniques for sport performers.

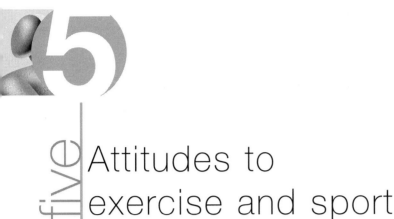

Attitudes to exercise and sport

Our beliefs can have a powerful effect on our behaviour. If you agree that participation in exercise and sport is valuable for your physical and mental well-being, then you have a positive attitude to exercise and sport. However, if you disagree, believing sport is damaging or stressful, you have a negative atitude and are unlikely to participate. Other beliefs are related to our explanations for our own behaviour, and for the behaviour of others. These are called our attributions. Our attributions and attitudes can have a powerful effect on sport performance and participation.

IN THIS CHAPTER WE WILL EXAMINE:

- theories of attribution and sport
- exercise, health and mental health
- burnout and withdrawal from sport.

Theories of attribution and sport

Attributions are the way people explain the causes of particular events or behaviours to themselves. Look at this extract from Linford Christie's (1995) autobiography:

> After losing at the World Championships in 1991, when I panicked as Carl Lewis came next to me, I decided I had to find some way of concentrating even more intensely so that I could block out everyone else (p.145).

Here Christie attributes losing the World Championships to insufficient concentration. As this was something he had control over, he felt he could do something about it. Knowing the attributions an athlete makes can help us understand:

- how to keep the athlete motivated
- the athlete's expectations about their own and others' abilities
- how to help the athlete improve performance
- how to achieve satisfaction with performance.

ATTRIBUTION THEORY

Attribution theory is an attempt to explain how we use information to come to conclusions about the causes of our own and other people's behaviour. Weiner (1972) proposed that achievement is related to the attributions we make. When he asked people why they had succeeded or failed on a task, he noted that their answers could be categorised as due to either:

- **internal** or **external** factors – internal are related to themselves; external to factors outside their control
- **stable** or **unstable** factors – stable factors are those which do not change; unstable factors are those which change or can be changed.

In Table 5.1 below you can see how the the internal/external dimensions and stable/unstable dimensions combine to produce four types of attribution. Let us put some flesh on this by imagining a sprinter who, like Linford Christie, has just lost a race. He may attribute his failure to one of the causes in Table 5.1.

• **Table 5.1:** The four types of attributions

	Internal Attribution	**External Attribution**
Stable Attribution	lack of talent	an 'unlucky' track
Unstable Attribution	lack of concentration	traffic jam

ATTRIBUTIONS AND PERFORMANCE

These attributions affect behaviour in a variety of ways, all of which have consequences for sports achievement. For example, if a sprinter explains his defeat as due to insufficient personal talent (an internal and stable cause) then he will make no effort to change. However, Linford Christie saw the cause as due to lack of concentration (internal and unstable) so he could do something about it. With this in mind, we will look at each dimension in turn, along with the effect on performance.

internal and external attributions

The internal–external dimension reflects the work of Julian Rotter (1966), who investigated people's beliefs about the extent to which they feel in personal control of what happens in their lives. Using the term **locus of control**, he proposed that those with an internal locus of control believe that what they do can influence outcomes. In contrast, those with an external locus of control believe that outcomes are influenced by external factors, such as luck, fate or other people.

Attributing outcomes to our own efforts can create emotions, such as pride: 'My preparation strategy really paid off' or shame: 'I let my coach down badly with that performance'. According to Weiner (1972), these emotions are an indicator of attributions. Internal attributions, such as effort, create more powerful emotions than external ones, such as luck. A speedskater who wins a race because she has beaten everyone else will show more exhilaration in her voice and body language than one who has won after the leading skater fell (the predominant emotion here will probably be relief).

Internalising success leads to increased self-confidence, but internalised failure may lead to shame, feelings of incompetence and eventual withdrawal, a topic which is covered in more detail towards the end of this chapter.

stable and unstable attributions

The stability of our attributions is based on past experiences ('We've lost to them in the last five matches') and therefore creates expectations about the future ('We'll probably lose this match too'). We anticipate the same outcomes if we hold stable attributions. What if, to our surprise, we win the sixth match? We would then be likely to attribute the cause to an unstable factor such as luck.

This is equally true if our past experience has been of success, but then we fail. We are likely to make an unstable attribution which may be external, such as bad line-calls, or internal, such as poor preparation. We would therefore expect a different outcome next time.

Weiner asserts that high and low achievers can be distinguished on the basis of their attributional patterns. Because high achievers attribute their success to internal reasons, and experience pride in their successes, they seek out more opportunities for success. In addition, because they attribute failure to unstable factors, they are more likely to persist after failure because they feel that it is possible to change. In contrast, low achievers tend to attribute failure to stable factors and therefore give up, as they think there is little they can do to change things. Of course they may be wrong! Errors in attributions will be discussed on p.71.

controllability and learned helplessness

Weiner added another dimension in 1979 – controllability (though as there is some debate about how this relates to the other two dimensions, it is less widely used). Where Rotter saw locus of control (see p.69), as a personality trait and therefore fairly permanent, Weiner viewed controllability as one of the ways in which we explain events. He divided controllability into personal control and external control.

If, for example, we attribute someone's failure to something beyond their control (called external control), we will blame them less and treat them more kindly than if we attribute their failure to a factor within their control (personal control).

• **Figure 5.1:** If the receiver makes an error in the change-over, the coach will be more critical if he attributes the error to something which is within the receiver's control

Most of us prefer to feel in control of our own destiny, not at the mercy of external forces or controlled and dictated to by others. When our freedom is threatened we react, but if our efforts to regain control continually fail, then **learned helplessness** may result. Seligman (1975) coined this term and briefly it means that the individual learns, by their repeated inability to change something, that failure is inevitable. Eventually they become passive and lose the motivation to act.

People vary in the degree to which they succumb to learned helplessness, depending on their beliefs as to why they are unsuccessful – in other words, depending on their attributions. If they attribute failure to an unstable factor then they are more likely to keep trying.

ERRORS IN ATTRIBUTIONS

Of course we are not always accurate in the attributions we make. Three of the commonest errors are:

- The **fundamental attribution error** – we tend to over-emphasise internal factors as the cause of someone's behaviour, rather than to the circumstances at the time. For example, we are more likely to attribute a poor dive as due to the diver's lack of practice, rather than her having difficulties getting to the competition, and thus feeling unprepared.
- The **self-serving bias** – we tend to explain behaviour or outcomes in ways which protect our self-esteem. For example, we attribute success to internal reasons ('we won because our passing was more accurate') and failure to external reasons ('we lost because of poor refereeing').

• **Figure 5.2:** In this example of the actor–observer effect, this fielder is likely to explain missing the ball as due to external reasons out of his control ('I dropped that catch because the sun was in my eyes'). However, an observer would attribute it to internal factors, which are within his control ('He dropped that catch because he wasn't concentrating').

Success is rarely attributed to refereeing! When Gill (1980) asked women basketball players about the reasons for their successes and failures, as expected players said that their successes were due to their team, whereas their failures were blamed on the other team. However, when she asked whether the result was due to themselves or their team-mates, members of winning teams attributed success to their team-mates, but members of losing teams attributed failure to themselves.

*   The **actor–observer effect** – researchers such as Nisbett *et al.* (1973) noted that attributions differ depending on whether we are the actor or the observer. The actor is likely to attribute his behaviour to external reasons, but an observer would attribute the behaviour to internal reasons. For an example see Figure 5.2.

Section summary Having looked at Weiner's way of categorising attributions, we have seen how these can be related to self-confidence, to emotions and to success. However, the main interest in attributions in sport is the way they influence the performer's behaviour. The performer's attributions affect their response to pressure, to difficulties, to failure and success. Attributions also affect our responses to others, as we noted in the section on controllability, and again in errors in attribution. These errors underline an important point. What matters is not whether the individual is right or wrong in their attributions, but how the attributions are classified.

Exercise, health and mental health

Although sport psychologists have been most interested in helping the sportsperson pursue their sports successfully, the research discussed below provides evidence for the health benefits for sports participants as well as those who exercise, perhaps by going running, working out in a gym or attending aerobics classes.

EXERCISE AND HEALTH

Regular exercise has a number of important benefits for health. It:

*   helps lower cholestrol, may reduce weight and lowers blood pressure, all of which (along with smoking) are the greatest risks for heart disease
*   seems to protect against osteoporosis because exercise helps to strengthen bones
*   maintains muscle strength and reaction time longer into old age, thus protecting balance and maintaining confidence in movement.

It is for these reasons that the Health Education Authority in the UK is aiming to increase the percentage of people aged 16–74 who take a minimum of at least 30 minutes moderate physical activity on five days of the week. In 1990 the percentage was 18 per cent, and the aim is to increase it to 90 per cent by 2005. For people who are already moderately active and fit, the aim is to increase their level to 20 minutes of vigorous exercise three times a week.

EXERCISE AND MENTAL HEALTH

The link between exercise and positive mental health has also been well documented. One of the measures used in research is the **Profile of Mood States** (POMS). This was devised by McNair, Lorr and Droppleman (1971) to measure a range of mood states: tension, depression, anger, vigour, fatigue, and confusion. Mood states are temporary, whereas personality traits are relatively permanent.

Morgan (1979) proposed a **mental health model** of exercise participation. He compared successful elite athletes with unsuccessful athletes, and the results showed a difference in their scores on the POMS, as you can see from Figure 5.3.

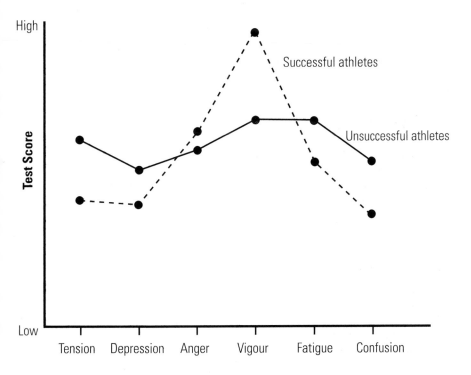

• **Figure 5.3:** Scores for athletes on the POMS

Whereas unsuccessful athletes show a similar score for all moods (which produces a fairly level line), the successful athlete's score on 'vigour' is well above that of the unsuccessful athlete, but scores on the other moods (tension, depression, anger, fatigue, confusion) are well below those of the unsuccessful athlete. In other words, the successful athlete scores higher on the positive mood and lower on the negative moods – the mental health model. However this does not always hold true – as we will see, overtraining produces a very different profile (see p.76).

Research on non-athletes has shown that even 30 minutes of running or cycling results in a change in a participant's Profile of Mood States. The profile shows an increase in vigour and a reduction in negative elements such as tension and anxiety. However Berger, Friedmann and Eaton (1988) proposed that these benefits are short-lived. Exercise levels must be maintained to have long-term benefits.

The psychological benefits of physical activity on mentally healthy individuals are well substantiated, according to a review of the literature by Leith and Taylor (1990), but it seems to have an even greater effect on people diagnosed as suffering from anxiety or depression. There are several explanations for this beneficial effect:

- increase in self-efficacy – as the individual continues exercising or participating in sport, their sense of mastery, skill and accomplishment develops
- interaction with others – exercise or sport frequently involves associating with other people, which may be pleasurable
- distraction from other concerns – this enables the exerciser to forget about worries, although it may only be a temporary distraction
- increased production of neurotransmitters – people suffering from depression often secrete low levels of neurotransmitters such as serotonin and dopamine; exercise increases the production of these chemicals
- as the individual is already at a low level of mental health, improvements are likely to be greater than in the mentally healthy person.

Theme link to Perspectives and Issues (**approaches in psychology**)

The explanations listed above relate to different approaches in psychology. These approaches (listed alphabetically) are: cognitive, individual differences, physiological, social. At the end of this chapter, exercise 2 asks you to link each of the above explanations with one of these four approaches.

PARTICIPATION IN EXERCISE AND SPORT

Exercise is provided by participation in sports as well as many other activities. Exercise can be provided by a game of squash, swimming, aerobics, golf or brisk walking. The intensity of many physical activities can be varied to suit the individual's current level of fitness, physical health, ability and age.

Given the benefits outlined above, why do so few people participate in exercise activities? Sallis and Hovell (1990) proposed a framework for studying the answer to this question, and identified four phases:

- **Sedentary phase** – the individual does not take part in exercise
- **Adoption phase** – the individual begins to take regular exercise
- **Maintenance or drop-out phase** – the individual continues with exercise or drops out. The drop-out may go back to the sedentary phase or may go to the last phase.
- **Resumption phase** – the individual who dropped out resumes regular exercise.

Using this framework the researchers studied what factors (or determinants) influence the individual to move from one phase to the next. Research by Sallis *et al.* (1986) looked at adults who did not participate in exercise and followed them up a year later. Results showed that those who took up vigorous exercise (moving from the sedentary to the adoption phase) were generally confident they could succeed at a vigorous exercise program (an example of self-efficacy). Self-efficacy seems to be more important than self-motivation in maintaining such a programme, according to Garcia and King (1991). They also tended to have high levels of self-control, were fairly knowledgeable about healthy lifestyles and the value of exercise, and were not usually overweight or obese.

These factors also affect the likelihood of an individual moving from the adoption to the maintenance phase, as do other factors, such as the support of a spouse, adequate time, access to sporting facilities and high risk of heart disease. Factors determining drop-out include being overweight, smoking and type of occupation. Withdrawal from sport is considered in more detail in the final section of this chapter.

Section summary

This section has identified some of the physical and mental benefits of participation in exercise. We have considered some reasons why people take up, and stay with, a vigorous exercise programme, and also why they drop out. There is still much work to be done in this area before these questions can be answered, but, until they are, a significant proportion of the population may fail to enjoy the physical and mental benefits of exercise.

Burnout and withdrawal from sport

People participate and then withdraw from their sports activities for a variety of reasons. We will start by looking at burnout, which is more likely to occur in elite athletes. Given the health benefits documented earlier in this chapter, researchers are also investigating why those who are involved at a recreational level withdraw from sports. We will see how knowledge of people's attitudes to sport may contribute to an explanation.

BURNOUT

Burnout results from the intense level of training which elite participation requires. It is the exhaustive psycho-physiological response to repeated unsuccessful efforts to meet the demands of training stress (Silva 1990). Accordingly, there are both physiological and psychological symptoms of burnout. As you will see, they are the opposite of the benefits which have been found in exercise participation.

Physiological symptoms of burnout include increased heart rate and blood pressure, chronic muscle fatigue, increased presence of biochemical indicators of stress and an increase in colds and infections.

Psychological symptoms of burnout include increased mood disturbances, decreased self-esteem, increased exhaustion and more negative interactions with others. Morgan *et al.* (1987) reviewed POMS scores (see p.73) for swimmers and noted that as the training demands became heavier there were changes in the swimmers' moods. Swimmers who were overtrained showed the opposite pattern, their vigour decreased and the negative mood states of tension, depression and fatigue increased.

It appears that high levels of training do not improve performance when compared to moderate levels. For example, Costill *et al.* (1991) reported that swimmers who trained for two 1.5 hour sessions per day showed the same level of improvement as those who trained for one 1.5 hour session per day. Both groups trained for six weeks. This suggests that high levels of training should be avoided, as they bring little benefit and put the athlete at risk of burnout.

Silva (1990) proposed the following stages in the process leading to burnout and withdrawal:

- **staleness** – if increased training fails (or appears to fail) to produce any gain, then staleness results. Staleness is the initial failure of the body to adapt to training stress.
- **overtraining** – if the athlete fails to 'train through' the staleness and improve performance, then he will experience overtraining. A brief respite from training at this point may prevent the burnout process continuing.

- **burnout** – the athlete who fails to cope with the effects of overtraining may eventually experience burnout, which is complete mental and physical exhaustion.
- **withdrawal** – withdrawal from the situation is the best solution, and almost inevitable according to Silva. This allows the athlete complete physical and mental rest.

In another explanation for burnout, Schmidt and Stein (1991) put forward an **investment model** of commitment to sport. They propose that athletes remain committed to their sport because of their enjoyment of it or their personal investment in it. Enjoyment includes personal satisfaction and rewards, and few costs (low levels of stress). In contrast, the athlete who gains little reward or satisfaction from their involvement but experiences increasing stress may continue mainly because they have invested so much time, effort and expense in their sport. This athlete will see few alternatives, will feel trapped and will be a likely candidate for burnout, according to Schmidt and Stein.

WITHDRAWAL FROM SPORT

At a lower level of expertise, teachers, coaches, parents, health professionals and psychologists have been concerned about the level of withdrawal from sport. In the previous section we noted some of the reasons why people drop out of exercise programmes. Here we focus on withdrawal from sport, by considering how a person's attitudes can affect their behaviour.

attitudes and sport

Secord and Backman (1964) proposed that attitudes have three components, known as the ABC of attitudes:

- **Affective** component – what we feel about a person, activity or object (I enjoy playing badminton).
- **Cognitive** component – what we believe about the activity, person or object (I think badminton improves my physical skills and fitness).
- **Behavioural** component – what I do, or intend to do in relation to the activity, person or object (I play badminton regularly).

As my beliefs and feelings are positive, my behaviour is likely to be positive. In other words, I take part in badminton. But if my feelings or beliefs changed, then my behaviour could change, leading to my withdrawal from badminton. From this perspective there are two ways in which withdrawal might be prevented. The first is to encourage strong positive attitudes to sports participation which will be more resistant to change. The second is to try to change negative attitudes to positive ones. Both of these options are described briefly below.

attitude formation

Attitudes are largely developed through experiences such as those listed below. Some examples of how positive attitudes to a sport may develop are:

- **familiarity** or **availability** of an activity, such as frequent exposure to a sport at school or with family or friends. Zajonc (1968) found that frequent exposure was related to positive attitudes.
- **positive associations**, such as having fun, learning new skills, being part of a group or winning approval from others. Gill, Gross and Huddleston (1983) asked young people why they participated in sports activities. The main reasons given were to learn and improve skills, to win or achieve, being with friends, and being part of a group or team.
- **social influences**, such as hearing positive comments from influential others like teachers, sports stars, parents or peers.

changing negative attitudes

Attitude change has been the subject of much research and is of interest to those working in advertising, politics and health care, as well as in sport. The relationship between attitude and behaviour does not appear to be strong, and attempts to change behaviour by changing attitudes are plagued with difficulties. One aspect which seems to make attitude change more likely is when the attitude is specific. For instance, Gill (1986) distinguishes between a negative attitude to rugby (specific) and to sports (general).

As our focus here is on the individual's withdrawal from a sport in which they have previously participated, it should be possible to be specific and identify what part of their attitude has changed. Consider the research by Weiss and Petlichkoff (1989). They reviewed the reasons young athletes gave for withdrawal from sport. The most common reasons included:

- pressure from coach and parents
- lack of fun
- lack of improvement
- conflict of interest and time.

Some of these reasons can be explained in terms of withdrawal of **reinforcement**, which leads to **extinction** of behaviour. However they can also be related to a change in attitude. A child who enjoyed going to judo sessions with her friends might come under pressure from the instructor to practise harder or show more commitment. Judo is no longer fun, so the affective component of the girl's attitude becomes negative. This influences her behaviour and she withdraws.

   Some of the topics covered elsewhere in this book may explain why people withdraw from sport. These include extrinsic/intrinsic motivation (p.41), attribution (p.68), leadership and coaching (p.101), motivation and self-confidence (p.38). Each of these may be considered in terms of the individual's attitude to sport.

Section summary

This final section has considered reasons why people experience burnout and why they withdraw from sport. We have touched on the elite athlete, the novice and the young participant. A consistent thread seems to be the individual's own attitude, whether it relates to self-confidence, attributions of success or failure, or the benefits they perceive from their participation. The development of strongly held and positive attitudes in childhood may reduce the chances of later withdrawal from sport.

KEY TERMS

actor–observer effect
attitude
(affective/behavioural/cognitive)
attribution
burnout
extinction
fundamental attribution error
internal–external attribution
investment model
learned helplessness
locus of control
mental health model
overtraining
Profile of Mood States
reinforcement
self-serving bias
stable–unstable attribution
staleness
withdrawal

Below are six imaginary responses given by sportspeople after success or failure. Draw up a table showing the four types of attribution (see Figure 5.1) and put each response into the correct slot.

After success: 'Our supporters are fantastic'
                  'I managed to conquer my nerves'
                  'The two internationals weren't in the
                  competition'
After failure: 'I didn't feel prepared'
                  'As a team we're not so together when we
                  play at high altitude'
                  'I just don't have the stamina'

Turn to page 74, Link each of the four approaches given in the Theme Link box to one explanation for improvements in mental health.

3. Think of a sport towards which you have a positive attitude and one towards which you have a negative attitude. Break down both attitudes into their affective, behavioural and cognitive components. Describe each component.

1. Discuss the benefits of participation in exercise or sport.

2. Describe the key features of attribution theory and discuss how they could be used to improve an athlete's performance.

3. Consider ways in which you might reduce an individual's likelihood of withdrawal from either a sport or from an exercise programme.

Further reading

Biddle, S. J. H. (Ed) (1995) *European Perspectives on Exercise and Sport Psychology*. Champaign, IL: Human Kinetics Publishers (Chapters 2, 3, 4, and 5).

Cox, R. H. (1998) *Sport Psychology: Concepts and Applications* (4th ed.). Boston, MA: WCB McGraw-Hill (Chapters 7 and 10).

Gill, D. L. (1986) *Psychological Dynamics of Sport.* Champaign, IL: Human Kinetics Publishers (Chapter 10).

Horn, T. S. (Ed) (1992) *Advances in Sport Psychology*. Champaign, IL: Human Kinetics Publishers (Chapter 5).

Morris, T. and Summers, J. (Eds) (1995) *Sport Psychology – Theory, Applications and Issues*. Milton, Queensland: John Wiley & Sons (Chapter 5 and 11).

Kremer, J. and Scully, D. (1994) *Psychology in Sport.* London: Taylor & Francis (Chapter 6).

Pargman, D. (1998) *Understanding Sport Behaviour.* Upper Saddle River, NJ: Prentice Hall, Inc. (Chapters 5 and 6).

Wann, D. L. (1997) *Sport Psychology*. Upper Saddle River, NJ: Prentice Hall, Inc. (Chapter 9).

Websites

http://www.mindtools.com/burnout.html – advice to the sportsperson on how to deal with and avoid burnout.

http://www..as.wvu.edu/**sbb/comm221/chapters/attrib.htm – more information on attribution.

http://www.ideafit.com/ftapril.htm – ten tricks for sticking to exercise, using a variety of psychological strategies.

six Social influence in sport

Social psychology involves the study of the individual in a social situation, which is a key feature of sport. The sprinter performs alone, whereas the hockey player depends on team-mates. Nevertheless both performs alongside others and in front of an audience. What effect do they have on the performer and why?

IN THIS CHAPTER WE WILL EXAMINE:

- group cohesion and performance
- effects of an audience on performers
- home advantage and audience characteristics.

Group cohesion and performance

When studying existing groups, psychologists consider that the chief features are: feelings of interpersonal attraction between members; a collective identity in which they view themselves as a unit, distinct from other groups; and a sense of shared purpose. In sport the purpose of a group is to achieve certain objectives which may be very explicit. Group members depend on each other in order to achieve these objectives.

In a sport setting the group may be a hockey team, a tennis club, a group of climbers or a national sport association. In other words, they may be a team, clearly defined with positions and roles to play, or they may be an informal group. However the word 'team' is sometimes used to denote a very strong group. A group goes through four stages of development, according to Tuckman (1965):

- **forming** – initially team members get to know each other, work out whether they feel they belong to the group and what part they will play. This is the stage when players start to test their relationships with others in the group.

- **storming** – this stage occurs when conflict develops between members and, in particular, rebellion against the leader. Members are jockeying to establish their roles and status.
- **norming** – co-operation starts to replace conflict. Members start working towards common goals. **Group cohesion** develops which improves individual satisfaction within the group and may also improve the success of the group. There is increasing mutual respect for each member's individual contribution.
- **performing** – this stage is achieved when roles and relationships have stabilised and the primary goal for each member is group success.

GROUP COHESION

Henry Tajfel (1978) asserted that humans have a natural tendency to categorise themselves and others into groups. This claim is based on research such as that summarised in the Core Study box below. Furthermore, in his **social identity theory**, Tajfel argues that we are biased in this way in order to maintain our self-esteem. According to this view then, once we are part of a group we will stick together and protect our group's interests.

> **Core study – Experiments in intergroup discrimination**
>
> Tajfel (1970) tested the extent to which 14- and 15-year-old schoolboys would favour those in their own group rather than those in another group. The boys already knew each other, and were told they had been put into one of two groups on the basis of their ability to estimate a number of dots. When asked to award points to the other boys, they favoured the boys who were in their group.
>
> Tajfel's point is that even when there is no competition between groups, and when membership of a group is based on minimal differences between people, members of a group will favour their own group members (the **in-group**) and discriminate against the others (members of the **out-group**). This tendency to act in favour of one's own group is a basis for group cohesiveness.

Athletes report that team cohesion is a source of satisfaction in their lives, yet there is conflicting evidence as to whether the most cohesive teams are the most successful. Sport psychologist Albert Carron (1982) has distinguished between two aspects of group cohesion:

- **task cohesion** – the degree to which group members work together and are committed to achieving common goals
- **social cohesion** – the degree to which group members like each other and get on, trust and support each other.

These two aspects, or dimensions, are independent of each other, so you might be very committed to achieving the goals of your team, but not particularly attached to the other members of the team. A team in which members get on well and are very committed to achieving common goals (at the performing stage of group development) may be successful, but equally a team in which there are major disputes (at the storming stage) may do as well if there is a high commitment to the common goal. A definition of cohesion which incorporates these ideas was proposed by Carron (1982): 'a dynamic process which is reflected in the tendency for a group to stick together and remain united in the pursuit of its goals and objectives' (p.124).

factors associated with group cohesion

The following factors seem to be associated with group cohesion:

- group size – smaller groups are more cohesive than larger ones, possibly because there is greater opportunity to interact, but also because there may be less chance for faulty group processes to occur (see next section).
- external threats – the presence of external threats increases group cohesion, perhaps because they force members to ignore internal divisions.
- similarity of members – cohesiveness is increased if members have equal status in the group, similar characteristics (such as age, skill level) and have been members for some time.
- stability in the members of the group – greater stability allows time for relationships between members to develop.
- success – successful performance is related to high group cohesion.

Although these factors are associated with group cohesion, the nature of this association is not at all clear. Does satisfaction with team members lead to success as a team which in turn increases group cohesion, or is it successful performance which increases team cohesion? Psychologists have tried to tease apart the relationships, but with little success to date.

group norms

One of the defining features of a group is that it has common beliefs, usually unspoken, about what is acceptable, unacceptable and how things are done: these are the **group norms**. As the group develops through the stages described on pp.83-4, group norms develop. Each member shows his or her commitment to the group by conforming to these norms. Those who challenge the norms also challenge the group's solidarity, hence groups exert pressure on their members to conform to the norms. The leader or leaders of a group have a particular responsibility here – part of their role is to set, maintain and enforce group norms. Such norms may include dress, attitude to training, post-match behaviour and treatment of new members.

• **Figure 6.1:** This team's norm for celebrating success will increase group cohesion

FACTORS AFFECTING GROUP PERFORMANCE

A good team is more than a group of skilled players. They need to work together effectively to be successful. Steiner (1972) has proposed that this can be expressed as:

actual productivity = potential productivity − losses due to faulty group processes

This suggests that, in order to improve team performance, coaches need to increase the skills and performance of individual players (potential productivity) whilst reducing faulty group processes, some of which are reviewed below.

group roles

Every group has members who take on certain roles, either formally or informally. A **role** is the set of behaviours expected of a person in a certain position. Formal roles are those which are part of the structure of a group. As an example, a goalkeeper has different responsibilities, different skills and relates to other members of the team in a different way from the coach.

A team will be more effective if players know what the roles are, they know who is responsible for what, they can see how each of them fit into the team picture and have an appreciation of the tasks of others, as well as their own. A player who accepts his role will be more committed and put in more effort. Lack of role acceptance can lead to poorer performance and can also damage group cohesion.

Informal roles are those which are not officially part of the structure but which help the group function. A player who is good at soothing conflict and bringing people together may act as a mediator. Someone who has been in the team for a long period may take on the role of 'mentor' towards new members. Not all roles make a positive contribution to the group – there may be a troublemaker who engenders conflict, or a member with a strong personality who gathers a group of 'followers' and forms a powerful sub-group or clique. However, other members of the group know who plays these roles, and one of the tasks of new members is to find out who performs the unofficial roles.

social loafing

Social loafing is the term used by Latané *et al.* (1979) for the reduced effort that the individual exerts when working with others. It is also known as the **Ringelmann effect**, because in the late 19th century Ringelmann measured the amount of effort men put into a tug-of-war task. He found that the more men were pulling, the less effort each individual put in. Generally, an individual's effort when performing with one other person is about 90 per cent of his effort when performing alone, and with seven others it is about 50 per cent.

Some possible explanations for this drop in effort are that the individual thinks that:

- the others are not fully committed and does not want to be the 'sucker'. Men seem to dislike the 'sucker' role more than women. When the performer feels that the others are putting in the same amount of effort, then motivation increases.
- his own effort is not recognised because it cannot be identified. Latané *et al.* (1980) showed that when effort is directly monitored and evaluated, social loafing does not occur. They created a simulated swim meet with spectators, trophies and competitors. All swimmers took part in individual and in relay events and laps were timed. When they were told lap times were not going to be announced, competitors swam slower in the relay than as individuals. However, when times were to be announced the swimmers were faster in the relay than in the individual events.
- the others will cover up for the lack of effort. Research shows that when the outcome has personal importance to the individual they will increase their effort regardless of the others.

- his own efforts will make little difference to the outcome. Commitment increases when the individual is convinced that their effort will make a difference to the outcome.

These findings have consequences for coaches – for example, one of the cliches in sports is 'There is no 'I' in team'. However, research on social loafing shows that coaches ignore the 'I' at their peril. Coaches are therefore advised to provide feedback on performance both to individuals and to the group as a whole.

It appears that social loafing is a predominantly Western phenomenon related to our individualist culture. In collectivist cultures the opposite occurs, and this is called **social striving**. Triandis (1990) noted that in collectivist cultures people pay much more attention to their in-group, and in-group goals are considered more important than individual goals.

arousal

Maintaining the appropriate level of **arousal** in a group affects performance. Zander (1975) proposed that desire for group success is at its maximum when the group has challenging but realistic goals. This is achieved by operating at a 50 per cent chance of success. Therefore, when a team meets very strong opposition arousal will be high and members reduce this by increasing their confidence and 'talking up' the chances of success. Conversely, if the competitive situation is not very challenging, the coach or leader must 'talk up' the chances of failure in order to increase arousal.

As discussed in Chapter 4, generally raising arousal may benefit some players but lead to over-arousal in others. The coach or captain needs to be aware of each team member's optimal level of arousal in order to avoid over-arousal.

co-ordination

Co-ordination refers to the degree to which each player's skills are meshed together as tightly as possible. This is a particularly important feature of **interactive sports** such as soccer, rugby and volleyball. In sports such as these coaches will design training sessions which include practice in passing, timing and the pattern of players' movements, in order to improve team co-ordination. In contrast, **co-active sports** such as swimming or golf suffer less from co-ordination problems.

group cohesion

Using Carron's distinction between task cohesion and social cohesion, research shows that successful performance depends on task cohesion but not so much on social cohesion. Overall though, it depends on the type of sport involved. Success in interactive sports such as soccer, where team

• **Figure 6.2:** If these hockey players have not practised co-ordination, this may damage their performance as a team

members rely on each other to perform successfully, seems to depend on team cohesion even more than the skill level. However, in sports which are co-active (such as swimming) individual performance is not dependent on others, and here the degree of cohesion has little effect on performance.

As mentioned earlier, it is unclear whether cohesion increases success or success increases cohesion. Overall there seems to be stronger evidence that performance affects cohesiveness, rather than cohesiveness affecting performance.

Section summary

This section has shown that ideas on the formation and cohesiveness of groups are very applicable to the sports setting. The focus has been on the functioning of teams and team performance. On some occasions social cohesion is more important than task cohesion, but the overall team activity is aimed at achieving a goal. Factors have been identified which can interfere with group performance, although research has been unable to determine whether success improves group cohesion, or cohesion increases the likelihood of success.

Effects of an audience on performers

If you have ever been in a situation where you have performed better when other people are watching, you have experienced **social facilitation**. Many of us have also had the opposite experience, when skills we can perform adequately suddenly fall apart when we are watched by others. Here, the presence of other people causes impairment of a task.

For the sportsperson, the fact that the presence of others may improve or impair performance is of considerable importance. Explanations for the **audience effect** which have been offered by psychologists have been based on research in a non-sports setting, but they nevertheless have a direct bearing on sport situations. We will review some of these explanations before considering some specific sport settings.

ZAJONC'S DRIVE THEORY OF SOCIAL FACILITATION

Robert Zajonc's (1965) theory is based on the effects of arousal (covered in more detail in Chapter 4) and explains how the presence of other people can lead to:

- **task enhancement** – improved performance on a simple task or one which is well-learned.
- **task impairment** – damaged performance on a complex task or one which has not been learned well.

According to **drive theory** (see p.51), as a skill becomes well-learned it requires less and less drive (or arousal) to be performed. Zajonc proposed that the presence of others increases our arousal, which in turn improves our performance of the well-learned task. In contrast, when we are performing a newly learned skill or complex task, our arousal level is already high. The additional arousal provided by an audience leads to **overload**, and this damages our performance.

Critics of this explanation argue that even on well-learned tasks a skilled athlete may perform poorly in front of others. Also, in a sports setting the audience is not merely watching, but is actively responding, so we must take into account how the presence of other people affects the performer.

COTTRELL'S EVALUATION APPREHENSION THEORY

Cottrell (1968) argued that arousal is caused not so much by the presence of others as by the apprehension of being evaluated by others – a form of social anxiety. Social approval or disapproval depends on the way others evaluate us, so if we are not confident, then we will be constantly worrying about how others are evaluating us. For example, a gymnast who is not completely confident of her routine may perform it well when watched by her family.

However, when performing in front of a panel of judges, she is more likely to make errors.

Cottrell showed that the more expert an audience was, the more a performance was impaired. His theory explains why performance deteriorates in the presence of an audience, but it is less successful at explaining why, at other times, it is enhanced.

BARON'S DISTRACTION-CONFLICT THEORY

Baron (1986) presented a cognitive explanation of social facilitiation. Using the idea that we have limited capacity to attend to information at any one time, he argued that we need little attention to perform an easy task but more for a complex one. However, the presence of others also demands our attention, and this creates additional and competing demands. It is this conflict between the competing demands of the task which increases arousal and thus leads to either improvement or impairment of performance, as shown in Figure 6.3.

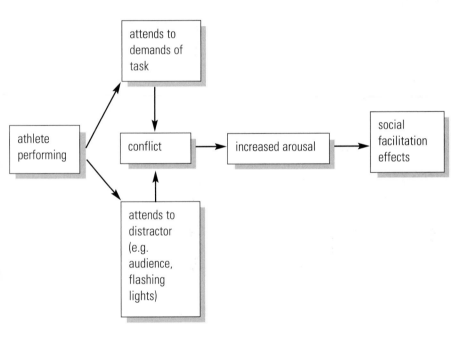

• **Figure 6.3:** Baron's model of distraction-conflict theory

Baron proposed that anything that distracts us will create conflict and so increase arousal, a theory which he demonstrated in a study using flashing lights as a distractor. Results showed that the flashing lights produced the same effect as an audience, namely that performance on easy tasks was improved and performance on difficult tasks was impaired. This suggests that one way for the sports performer to prevent himself from becoming over-aroused is to direct his attention to the task in hand and block out his awareness of others. This is covered in more detail in the section on selective attention and attentional narrowing (pp.111–13).

Section summary All three explanations for the audience effect identify arousal as a key factor. Although Baron shows that it is arousal – rather than the meaning that the arousal has – he cannot successfully account for Cottrell's findings that the impairment of the task is related to the level of expertise of the audience. However, all of these explanations are based on a passive audience, whereas sportspeople may perform in front of a partisan or hostile audience. This is the topic in the final section.

Home advantage and audience characteristics

Most of the research of active audiences in a sports setting has been focused on the **home advantage** effect. Does playing in front of the home crowd improve or impair performance? Research findings suggest that:

- for the major sports in the US surveyed by Schwartz and Barsky (1977), teams win more home matches than away matches (between 53–64 per cent are home wins).
- this research also showed that the home advantage was due to audience support. It is not due to the effects of travel on the visiting team, according to Courneya and Carron (1991).
- a home advantage may be more important in the early rounds of competition.

The home team advantage also has been found in football and rugby, and even in the Olympic Games. Leonard (1989) reported that the Olympic host country wins more medals than in Olympic games before or after.

EXPLANATIONS FOR THE HOME ADVANTAGE

Research suggests that it is the supportive audience which explains the home advantage, but a possible explanation for this effect comes from Varca (1980). He looked at the audience effect in terms of the home and the visiting team. From his study of basketball in the US, he classified aggressive play in two ways:

- **functional aggressive behaviour** – attacking play within the rules, play which benefited performance
- **dysfunctional aggressive behaviour** – play which contravened the rules, such as fouls, and which hampered performance

In principle there should be no difference in behaviour between the home team and the visiting team, but Varca analysed games over a season and found a significant difference between them in these two types of play. Home teams used more functional aggressive play and away teams more dysfunctional aggressive play.

Varca then proposed that the presence of the crowd increased arousal for both teams. Although this arousal led to improved performance for the home team, because of frustration, the visitors became more aggressive (as proposed in the **frustration–aggression hypothesis**, see p.26). In other words, the differences between the two teams could be as much due to away disadvantage as to home advantage. This effect has also been found in ice hockey.

AUDIENCE CHARACTERISTICS

Research has indicated that generally there is a home advantage, but what characteristics of the audience contribute to this? The following factors seem to be involved:

- **size** – there is some evidence that as the size of the crowd increases, arousal levels also increase. Schwartz and Barsky (1977) found that larger audiences were related to more home team wins in baseball.
- **intimacy** – Schwartz and Barsky (1977) also reported home advantages in American football, basketball and ice hockey. These last two sports have much smaller crowds than baseball and American football, so crowd size may not be a key factor. Edwards (1979) has proposed that the proximity of the supporters and players (which creates intimacy) has more influence on players than crowd size.
- **hostility** – a hostile crowd seems to have a negative influence on visiting teams. Greer (1983) studied basketball games in the US, monitoring players' performance for five minutes after periods of protest from fans. Interestingly these protests were often aimed at the officials, not the players. Nevertheless, results showed a slight improvement in the home players' performance, but a significant deterioration in the performance of the visiting team.

Section summary   The explanations for audience effects in mainstream psychology have been further developed through research in a sports setting. This has shown that there is a home advantage which seems to be directly related to the spectators. The evidence that it benefits the home team (unless the match is a crucial one) has been attributed to the differing effects of arousal. This arousal, and the hostility of the crowd, seem to improve the play of the home team and damage the performance of the visiting team. However, much of the research on the effect of audiences in sports has been conducted in the US on American sports. There is little research on the home advantage in other countries, or indeed on the sportsperson who performs alone.

KEY TERMS

arousal
audience effect
co-active sports
co-ordination
distraction-conflict theory
drive theory
dysfunctional aggressive play
evaluation apprehension theory
frustration–aggression hypothesis
functional aggressive play
group cohesion
group norms
home advantage
in-group
interactive sports
out-group
overload
Ringelmann effect
role
social cohesion
social facilitation
social identity theory
social loafing
social striving
task cohesion

EXERCISE **1**

Working in pairs, each pair must choose one of the following groups: a climbing club, an under-eleven football team, a judo club, a school hockey team, a tennis club, a professional basketball team, a swimming club. Look at the list of factors associated with group cohesion given on p.85. Relate each of the first four factors to your group and say what you would consider to be successful performance. Comparing notes with the other pairs, do you think there may be any other factors associated with group cohesion?

EXERCISE **2**

Which of the three theories of social facilitation is most appropriate for a sport setting? Give two reasons for your answer.

EXERCISE **3**

What can a visiting team do to counteract the effect of the home advantage?

ESSAY QUESTIONS

1. Discuss some of the factors which affect group cohesion.

2. Evaluate theories which explain the effects of an audience on performers.

3. Discuss the actions that a manager of a rugby club could take to prepare his players for an away match. Support your proposals with psychological research.

Further reading

Cox, R. H. (1998) *Sport Psychology: Concepts and Applications* (4th ed.). Boston, MA: WCB McGraw-Hill (Chapter 9).

Gill, D. L. (1986) *Psychological Dynamics of Sport*. Champaign, IL: Human Kinetics Publishers (Chapters 11 and 14).

Horn, T. S. (Ed) (1992) *Advances in Sport Psychology*. Champaign, IL: Human Kinetics Publishers (Chapter 8).

Morris, T. and Summers, J. (Eds) (1995) *Sport Psychology – Theory, Applications and Issues*. Milton, Queensland: John Wiley & Sons (Chapters 7, 8 and 16).

Kremer, J. and Scully, D. (1994) *Psychology in Sport*. London: Taylor & Francis (Chapter 6).

Pargman, D. (1998) *Understanding Sport Behaviour*. Upper Saddle River, NJ: Prentice Hall, Inc. (Chapter 12).

Wann, D. L. (1997) *Sport Psychology*. Upper Saddle River, NJ: Prentice Hall, Inc. (Chapter 14).

Websites

http://www.psywww.com/sports/cohesion.htm – advice on developing team cohesion in a sport setting.

http://www.cultsock.ndirect.co.uk/MUHome/cshtml/groups/groups.html – information on groups, cohesion and tasks.

seven

Leadership and coaching

Leaders play an important role in sports, whether as coach, captain of a team or manager of a club. They exert an influence on player satisfaction and individual or group successes. Are leaders born or made? What makes a good leader? Examination of leadership behaviour, and of the circumstances and people they lead, has enabled sport psychologists to help coaches, captains and managers to be more effective leaders.

IN THIS CHAPTER WE WILL EXAMINE:

- theories of leadership
- leadership styles and coaching styles
- coach–performer compatibility.

Theories of leadership

Leadership can be defined as the behaviour of an individual when he or she is directing the activities of a group towards a shared goal (Hemphill and Coons 1957). Below we consider leadership in terms of the personality traits of leaders, then leaders' behaviours, and finally the interactional approach. This approach also takes account of the situation in which the leader is operating.

THE GREAT MAN THEORY OF LEADERSHIP

Early research on leadership tried to identify which personality traits were common to successful leaders. This approach reflects the 'great man' theory, which suggests that some individuals are born to be great. They would emerge regardless of the circumstances, so a great leader in one sphere (say politics) would be equally good in another (sport perhaps.)

If great leaders have the same characteristics then this would suggest that people who have these characteristics would rise to positions of power and influence. There appeared to be some common traits amongst the leaders studied – from business, industry, politics and the military – for example they tended to be slightly more intelligent and dominant than their followers. However, differences did not add up to a clear 'great man' profile and could have been more related to how leaders emerge, rather than to how effective they are. So this approach (the trait approach) fell into disuse as researchers instead looked at what behaviours were associated with successful leadership.

THE BEHAVIOURAL APPROACH TO LEADERSHIP

Research into leadership behaviour by Lewin, Lippitt and White (1939), which is detailed later on pp.101–2, found that the behaviour of a group of boys depended on the behaviour of the leader. The leaders were taught to behave in particular ways, either authoritarian, democratic or laissez-faire, so it was their behaviour, not the leaders themselves, which made the difference.

The results of later work on leadership suggested that there are two aspects of leadership, such as Halpin (1966) proposed:

- **consideration** – leadership behaviours are focused on the members of the group or workforce, fostering good relations and an egalitarian attitude to others.
- **initiating structure** – leadership behaviours are focused on the task to be achieved, and on directing the group in order to achieve that task.

INTERACTIONAL THEORIES

Critics argued that the continued focus on the leader, rather than the situation in which leadership takes place, provided a limited view of leadership. Thus, an **interactional approach** to leadership developed, which took into account the leader, the situation at the time, the type of people who were being 'led', and the interaction between them. The interactional approach is examined in the work of both Fiedler and Chelladurai.

fiedler's contingency theory

Fiedler (1967) argued that effective leadership depends on (is contingent on) the extent that the individual's style fits the situation. He understood leadership style to be a fairly stable disposition (a personality trait), and, echoing the distinctions provided by Halpin above, he said that leaders are either **relationship-motivated** or **task-motivated**.

To identify whether a leader was relationship- or task-motivated, Fiedler measured the leader's attitude to the person they found it most difficult to work with (called the **least preferred co-worker** or LPC). Those who saw their least preferred co-worker in a fairly positive way tended to be more tolerant, considerate and relationship-motivated with group members. Leaders with a very negative attitude to their LPC tended to be controlling and dominant in relationships with group members, they were task-motivated.

Fiedler also proposed that leadership effectiveness is contingent upon three aspects of the leadership situation (situational variables), namely:

- **leader–member relations** – if there is a high level of liking and trust of the leader and the leader has confidence in the group, leader–member relations are good`.
- **task structure** – the task may be clearly structured (it is clear what the aim is, how it is to be achieved and who takes decisions) or the goal may be poorly defined or there may be several ways of achieving it.
- **position power** – the amount of power in the leader's position, the amount of organisational support and the reward or punishments that the leader can give.

When the the values in each of these circumstances are high (such as good relations or clear task structure), Fiedler predicted that the low LPC leader would be most effective, because they could focus on the task without worrying about group morale. Equally if all the values were low (such as an unstructured task and low power) the low LPC leader would need to be task focused in order to try to get the task completed, and would have little to lose by ignoring team-members' feelings.

In contrast though, the high LPC leader would be most effective when circumstances were moderately favourable. For example when the leader has little power or the task is unclear, good interpersonal relationships are important to get everyone pulling together and ensure that they are able to tolerate confusion in the task structure.

Critics argue that because Fiedler viewed the attitude to the LPC as a measure of a personality trait, this implies that leaders cannot change their style. However, it seems that to some extent they can. Other proposals from the interactional perspective have emphasised particular aspects of the leader–group–situation relationship. These focus on:

- **decision-making** – Vroom and Yetton (1973) proposed that leaders must consider the quality of the decision and its acceptance by the group. With this in mind, the leader either makes the decision with little consultation (autocratic), or delegates the decision to others (delegative), or includes the whole group (participatory).
- **maturity of group members** – Hershey and Blanchard (1969) note that when members are inexperienced the leader must be directive and provide emotional support, but when they are experienced the leader must allow members more autonomy.

chelladurai's multidimensional model of leadership

The work on leadership we have looked at so far has been generated as a result of research on leadership in the workplace. Whilst these ideas have clear implications for sport participants, there are differences. For example, the aim of the activity is usually fairly clear in sport. Also, members may have more choice about staying in the group or choosing the leader than those in a work setting.

Chelladurai (1978) asked: What is effective leadership in sports situations and how can it be measured? He proposed that the indicator of effective leadership should be performance outcomes and member satisfaction. Using an interactional approach he devised the **Multidimensional Model of Leadership** (MML). In this he argued that effective leadership emerges when certain types of leader behaviour are matched with the following three characteristics:

* **situational characteristics** (such as whether the opposition is strong or weak) – these will determine the required leader behaviour
* **leader characteristics** (such as the leader's level of experience, personality, whether goal- or relationship-oriented) – these will determine the leader's actual behaviour
* **group member characteristics** (such as their experience, sex, age and personality) – these will determine what kind of leader behaviour they prefer.

Chelladurai proposes that if all three of the leader's behaviours match each of the three characteristics, then member satisfaction and team performance will be high. In others words, if the coach does what is required in the situation, and this is what the athletes want the coach to do, this is effective leadership. Figure 7.1 shows how the elements in the model are related.

We can see how this model works by applying it to a specific example. Imagine an under-eleven boys soccer team playing their first match of the season. Many of them are new to the club and for a few it is their first experience of competition. How can the coach provide effective leadership? Looking at Chelladurai's model (Figure 7.1), the situational characteristics do not create pressure to win, so the required behaviour is to allow players to try out their skills and practice working for each other. The member characteristics are youth and inexperience, so the preferred behaviour from the coach should be encouraging and supportive. If the coach's actual behaviour fits these needs, then a high level of performance and satisfaction results. This is effective leadership according to Chelladurai's criteria.

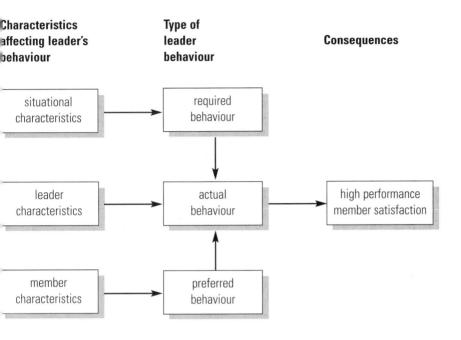

| Characteristics affecting leader's behaviour | Type of leader behaviour | Consequences |

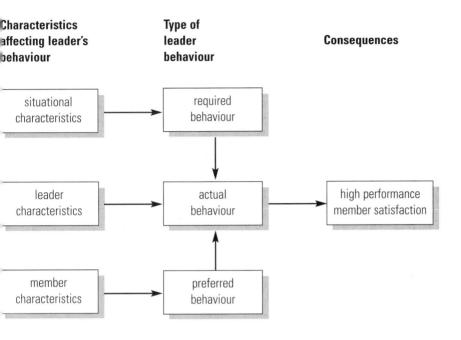

Figure 7.1: Chelladurai's multidimensional model of leadership

This model of leadership emphasises the need for flexibility in leaders. From the coach's viewpoint it ties in with teaching issues, where a more effective teacher or coach is one who can employ a range of teaching styles appropriately. This topic is discussed later in this chapter.

> **Section summary**
>
> Theories of leadership have moved away from the notion of innate leadership qualities and towards the awareness of the needs of the circumstances and the relationships with those led. Early research included leaders in hierarchical settings such as military, organisational or religious settings. The sport setting differs in that it may be more informal, and leaders may work with a few individuals (as well as with groups) who have more choice about working with the leader.

Leadership styles and coaching styles

In their research on leadership, Lewin, Lippitt and White (1939) identified three different styles of leadership behaviour and noted their effect on group performance. They studied adult leaders in boys' clubs and the behaviour of the boys (particularly aggression). The three styles were:

- **Authoritarian** or **autocratic style** – the leader dictates to the group who does what and how, and advice, ideas or comments are not asked for. Such leaders tend to be rather cool and impersonal and group members tended to be submissive in their attitude. Lewin found that when the leader was absent, group members tended to stop or slow down their work, and they became aggressive towards each other when things went wrong. Nevertheless they achieved results from their work, suggesting that this style is most valuable when a team is working towards a specific goal.
- **Democratic style** – the leader encourages the involvement of the individual members of the group, their ideas are listened to, and they are encouraged to participate in decisions related to the preparation and execution of group tasks. Nevertheless the leader makes final decisions and oversees the structure of group work. Lewin found that when the leader was absent, group members continued to work on their tasks and to co-operate when things went wrong, suggesting this style contributes to group cohesion. In general, this group were slightly less productive than the first group.
- **Laissez-faire style** – this style is really 'no leadership'. Laissez-faire means letting group members get on with things in their own way. Although leaders may help members get out of difficulties, they offer no direction or involvement. Lewin found members tended to be aggressive towards each other when things went wrong, gave up easily and were the least productive.

The requirements of the situation are the key to effective leadership, and the styles identified above have been developed in the teaching of sports skills, as you will now see.

TEACHING STYLES

Mosston and Ashworth (1986) have looked at the role of the teacher (or coach) and the learner in terms of decisions about what is taught/learned, when, how, and so on. The amount of influence the teacher and learner each has on these decisions can be classified and labelled on their **Spectrum of Teaching Styles**, which covers the range from autocratic to laissez-faire. At one end of the spectrum the teacher makes all the decisions (the command style); at the other end the learner makes most of them (the discovery style).

Below we examine four of the styles on this spectrum and the circumstances in which they are appropriate:

- **Command style** – the teacher has an authoritarian role, so this style can be used to control a group (such as a class of primary school children) or perhaps to convey the same information to all participants at the same time (for example in an aerobics group). All learners are treated in the same way and have very little influence on what is taught or how it is taught. Learners copy the teacher's behaviour or instructions and there is little opportunity for social contact between learners.

- **Reciprocal** or **paired style** – this style allows the learner to participate more actively in their learning. The teacher decides what is to be taught, but learners work together in pairs taking turns as the performer and the observer, analysing each other's performances and providing instant feedback. Everyone needs to know exactly what to do and should have some basic skills. The teacher's role here is to monitor what is happening, to give advice, support or to correct if necessary. However it requires careful monitoring to ensure that what the teacher has planned is being put into effect.
- **Problem-solving style** – here the teacher sets problems for the learners to solve, which encourages learners to think about their sport and to be creative in their approach to problems. There may be one solution or several, and the teacher may have limited control over how the learners work and think in order to solve the problem. This style is useful when there may be a number of possible options, or when the teacher wishes the learners to use information they have already learned but to apply and evaluate it in a novel situation. For example the teacher may ask 'how could you gain the attack if you were in this situation?' The learner may benefit from hearing others explain their ideas or thoughts, just as it helps their own understanding when they have to articulate their ideas and explain their thinking to others. The learner needs to have some experience within the sport, hence the problem-solving style is appropriate for the more skilled performer.
- **Discovery style** – here the teacher guides the learner by giving clues, hints and questions which get the learner to 'discover' ways of improving a skill or strategy. For example the teacher might say: 'Try it with your weight on the front foot, then with your weight equally distributed. Which is most effective? What situation could you use it in?' Here the teacher is a facilitator. There are similarities between this and the previous style, but this is a more creative and open-ended approach. This style is particularly appropriate to creative dance and some aspects of outdoor activities.

As the teaching style moves from teacher-centred to learner-centred, so the learner has greater control over, and involvement with, his or her learning. This has benefits in that it increases both intrinsic motivation and self-efficacy, enables the learner to remember and use learned skills more effectively and increases inter-personal skills. However it is only appropriate with certain age groups, on certain tasks, and in certain group sizes. A good coach will be skilled in the full range of teaching styles and deploy them appropriately.

• **Figure 7.2:** Which teaching style would have been appropriate for Canada's Kate Richardson, performing in the 2000 Olympics?

COACHING BEHAVIOURS

The study of coaches' behaviour, and its impact on players, enabled Smith, Smoll and Hunt (1977) to devise their **Coaching Behaviour Assessment System.** This allows researchers to analyse coaching behaviours by identifying twelve different categories, including whether coaching involves technical instruction, reinforcement, punishment or encouragement. The CBAS classified coaching behaviour in one of two ways:

- **reactive behaviours** – these are coaches' reactions to behaviours by the sportsperson. The reaction may be to a player's good performance, when the player makes a mistake, or when the player misbehaves.
- **spontaneous behaviours** – these are initiated by the coach and may either be related to the sport situation or irrelevant to the game.

Echoing Chelladurai's identification of what the player wants from a coach, research using the CBAS showed that the attitudes of players towards sport and to their teammates were related to their coach's behaviour. Indeed, Smoll and Smith (1989) noted that players are better judges of a coach's behaviour then the coach is.

Other studies of coaching behaviour using the CBAS have found that:

- children low in self-esteem respond well to encouragement, reinforcement and technical instruction (Smith and Smoll 1990)
- team cohesion is improved by positive feedback, social support and democratic behaviour on the part of the coach (Westre and Weiss 1991)
- players are less likely to drop out of their sport if the coach has attended a coaching effectiveness training programme (Barnett, Smoll and Smith 1992).

Information on leadership styles has been applied to the development of teaching styles in order to create more effective learning. The coach's role as leader and teacher can benefit from awareness of these styles. The CBAS, a tool for measuring various types of coaching behaviours, has helped sport psychologists improve coaching effectiveness by identifying coaching behaviours and changing them where necessary.

Section summary

Coach–performer compatibility

One of the themes running through this chapter is the relationship between the leader and the sportsperson. The quality of the relationship between a leader and group members influences the quality of the performance and the individual athlete's satisfaction, and this has been studied in some detail under the heading of **coach–performer compatibility**. Carron and Bennett (1977) studied coach–athlete pairs and identified three aspects of their relationship:

- **affection** – a close personal feeling between the two
- **control** – relates to authority, power and dominance
- **inclusion** – refers to good levels of communication and interaction between the performer and coach.

Of these three, the most important indicator of a compatible coach–performer pair was the last one. Highly compatible pairs were those with good quality communication. Incompatibility was evident where coach and performer were withdrawn or detached.

For their research, Fisher et al. (1982) devised a coding system of verbal and non-verbal behaviours by the coach. When players and coaches were assessed on their perceptions, results indicated that coaches of school teams whose members show high satisfaction tended to devise interesting and imaginative practice sessions, did not spend much time giving out information, but gave plenty of praise.

A further result from Fisher et al.'s research showed there was a disparity between the coach's perception of their own behaviour and the performer's perception. When rating themselves on various coaching behaviours (such as techniques or knowledge) coaches gave themselves higher ratings then those they were coaching. This difference in perceptions is borne out by other research, such as that by Smoll and Smith referred to on p.104. In a study of female volleyball coaches, Bird (1977) reported that the coaches thought they were task-oriented whereas their players thought they were more relationship-oriented. This difference in perceptions can contribute to poor compatibility between the coach and performer.

• **Figure 7.3:** A coach will be more effective if he can match his behaviour to the needs and ability of his players

Another element of coach–athlete compatibility relates to individual differences, such as the age or skill level of the sportsperson. Sport psychologists have studied which leadership or coaching style is best suited to a particular characteristic, finding the following factors to be significant:

- **Age** – young players, below the mid-teens, prefer a relationship-oriented approach with low task-oriented behaviours. In general the research shows that the older the athlete, the greater the preference for a leader who has an autocratic style, emphasises training and instruction but is socially supportive. This suggests that as a player gets older they prefer a more controlling style of leader, although this could be because older players were more skilled. Research on the age of players has generally not distinguished between their levels of skill, which may have confounded the results.
- **Gender** – female athletes prefer a democratic coaching style (which includes participation in decision-making) whereas males prefer an autocratic style. Horn and Glenn (1988) found that female athletes who were high in competitive trait anxiety (see p.58 for details) preferred coaches who provided support and positive feedback. Males' level of trait anxiety appeared to be unrelated to a preferred coaching behaviour. Differences in personality characteristics (such as level of self-confidence) between males and females may not be evident before puberty (12–13 years old), thus age interacts with gender and personality.
- **Ability level** – research is contradictory with regard to ability level. It seems that higher skilled athletes prefer a more relationship-oriented coach, whereas weaker players prefer a task-oriented approach because this focuses on instruction. However, research by Chelladurai and Carron (1983) found that skilled athletes preferred a more authoritarian style. This difference may be explained by the nature of the athlete's sport (such as team or individual), their level of expertise and the type of competition.

Section summary

This final section has looked at the relationship between coach and athlete, and further emphasises the variety of situations a coach may be in, and the flexibility he or she needs to employ in order to be effective for the sportsperson. Research suggests that both parties need to be able to communicate honestly and clearly, and the coach must give plenty of positive support. To be effective, coaches need to tailor their approach to suit individual differences such as age or skill level. They also need to be aware that their own view of their behaviour may be quite different from the players' view.

KEY TERMS

authoritarian/autocratic style
coaching behaviour assessment
    system (CBAS)
coach–performer compatibility
command style
democratic style
discovery style
Fiedler's contingency theory
great man theory
inclusion
interactional approach
laissez-faire style
leadership style
least preferred co-worker (LPC)
multidimensional model of
    leadership (MML)
problem-solving style
reciprocal/paired style
relationship-motivated
Spectrum of Teaching Styles
task-motivated

EXERCISE 1

Write down the three most important qualities of a good leader, in
your opinion. Then compare your answers with a partner and
decide on the four most important qualities. Would they apply to all
situations?

EXERCISE 2

Using Chelladurai's MML, describe what the situation and member
characteristics will be if a coach is preparing a team of under-
sixteen boys for the final of the inter-regional rugby competition.

Using either netball or basketball, link the four teaching styles listed on pp.102–3 to the development of a player's skill in shooting a goal.

ESSAY QUESTIONS

1. Consider an interactional model of leadership.

2. Evaluate the research on coach–performer compatibility.

3. Explain why team cohesion seems to be improved by positive feedback and democratic behaviour on the part of the coach.

Further reading

Cox, R. H. (1998) *Sport Psychology: Concepts and Applications* (4th ed). Boston, MA: WCB McGraw-Hill (Chapter 9).

Gill, D. L. (1986) *Psychological Dynamics of Sport.* Champaign, IL: Human Kinetics Publishers (Chapter 14).

Horn, T. S. (Ed) (1992) *Advances in Sport Psychology.* Champaign, IL: Human Kinetics Publishers (Chapter 9).

Pargman, D. (1998) *Understanding Sport Behaviour*. Upper Saddle River, NJ: Prentice Hall, Inc. (Chapter 14).

Wann, D. L. (1997) *Sport Psychology*. Upper Saddle River, NJy: Prentice Hall, Inc. (Chapter 13).

Websites

http://www.cultsock.ndirect.co.uk/MUHome/cshtml/groups/lead1.html – Lewin's leadership work and groups

http://www.coach.ca/tchart_e.htm – advice to coaches on how to be effective

eight

Attention and imagery in sport

If you have been talking with friends and suddenly hear someone speak your name, you have experienced your attentional processes at work. The study of how and what we notice (and almost notice) comes under the heading of cognitive psychology. Whilst early researchers studied our ability to attend to spoken information, more recently sport psychologists have looked at our ability to simultaneously attend to what we see, hear, think and do. This research provides ways of improving the sportsperson's performance.

IN THIS CHAPTER WE WILL EXAMINE:

- definitions and types of attention and imagery
- attention: measures, styles and strategies
- imagery and mental practice.

Attention – definitions and types

Attention has been defined by Hill (1998) as:

> the focusing and concentration of mental effort that usually results in conscious awareness of certain aspects of external sensory stimuli or mental experiences (p. 57).

There is a vast amount of sensory information coming into the brain at any one time. A footballer sees opposition players as well as team-mates, must note their movements, speed, direction, the position of the ball, the distance between players and ball, positions on the pitch, hear instructions from team mates, the manager, the referee's whistle, the crowd. He will also hear his own breathing, or the sound of a passing train, the sight of billboards and lights in the stadium, the feel of the ground under his feet, and the sense of his own muscle movements and balance.

It is not possible for the human brain to fully process all this information at once. Nevertheless, even the novice player can attend to some of the information and make appropriate moves. How does he do this? Psychologists have looked at attention in terms of how we select information to attend to (**selective attention**), and how we use the attentional resources we have (**attentional capacity**).

SELECTIVE ATTENTION

The process of picking out and focusing on information is called selective attention. Information not selected is filtered out. It seems that we cannot attend to two lots of similar information when presented at the same time. Cherry (1953) showed that participants attending to one spoken message noticed very little about another message presented at the same time. This message seemed to be at the periphery of their consciousness. However if one person is speaking whilst music is playing, we will be more succesful in attending to both sources – we will be able to attend to more information.

Several models have been proposed to explain how, and at what stage, we selectively attend to certain information whilst at the same time being able to move our attention to more important information when necessary. The situation of hearing your name whilst talking with friends is an example of this.

• **Figure 8.1:** Denmark's Camilla Martin is able to reach this shot because she can select the relevant information to attend to

As yet there is no satisfactory explanation for selective attention, but our ability to select, or focus, is useful in the sport situation. This is one way the athlete can filter out awareness of the crowd, or of fellow competitors in a race. For example, by focusing attention on the sound and rhythm of his breathing, everything else fades into the background (or attenuates).

Selective attention also helps the sportsperson to respond rapidly by being proactive, and looking for particular information. So, a badminton player will look at the angle of the opponent's racket as it strikes the shuttlecock, and by selecting this information can anticipate the flight of the shuttlecock.

Despite these examples, sportspeople often find it difficult to select the relevant information from the array of constantly changing information they receive. This is most true of the beginner, and particularly youngsters. As the individual gains in skill their attentional abilities become more efficient, which is the point we turn to now.

CAPACITY THEORY OF ATTENTION

In his capacity theory of attention, Kahneman (1973) proposed that there is a limited amount of attentional capacity available at any one time. He proposed the notion of a central allocation policy, which divides attention so it can meet the demands being made on it at any one time. This allocation of attentional resources occurs continuously, because demands, and their importance to us, are constantly changing. These aspects of the theory are discussed below, with particular regard to the sports setting.

arousal and attentional narrowing

The attentional capacity that we have at any one time is related to our level of arousal. Kahneman proposed that when we are lethargic our capacity is low, but it increases as arousal increases. This partly explains the value of arousal to effective performance. However, if arousal continues to increase it begins to have a damaging effect and research within sport psychology has contributed to our understanding of what happens.

Landers, Qi and Courtet (1985) studied the relationship between arousal, attention and performance, finding that at a low level of arousal the performer picks up both appropriate and inappropriate cues. At this level, the performer has a broad **attentional field**, just like the footballer described on p.111, and will not perform well. As his arousal increases, his attention narrows and the irrelevant cues are ignored. This **attentional narrowing** enables him to focus on relevant cues and so he performs well.

However, if arousal continues, his attention continues to narrow and his performance will deteriorate. There may be several reasons for this deterioration:

- too much arousal may undermine the athlete's ability to narrow his **attentional focus**.
- arousal increases immediately before the performance of a skilled motor task, such as in rifle shooting, archery and putting in golf as shown by Landers *et al.* (1985). This causes additional attentional narrowing which seems to damage performance of skilled motor tasks, a point discussed further in Chapter 4 on arousal (p.52).
- attentional narrowing causes the player to scan the attentional field less often or use his dominant **attentional style**, rather than several attentional styles as the occasion demands (see p.116 for details of attentional style).

Although the effects of attentional narrowing create a handicap for our footballer, who needs to be aware of all that is happening around him, it is advantageous to the gymnast because a narrow attentional focus enables her to shut out distractions.

demands on attention

The more skilled we are at a task the fewer attentional resources we need. When learning to play tennis the beginner has to attend to the weight of the racket in her hand, the bounce and speed of the ball, how to make the racket hit the ball and possibly advice from the tennis coach. She does not have the attentional capacity to meet all these demands, and might not even hear the coach speaking. After repeated attempts, she can swing the racket and judge the ball better so these tasks need less attention. She then has the capacity to attend to her movements in relation to the ball, and maybe to hear her coach's advice. When a task can be performed without any conscious mental effort, we are not using our attentional resources. This is known as **automatic processing**.

Overload occurs when the demands of the situation are greater than the amount of attention, as described for our novice tennis player – there is simply too much information for her to process. According to Kahneman's model, the role of the central allocation policy is to decide which tasks should receive more attention, but it is not clear how this works. Research has shown that if a sportsperson has too many attentional demands they are likely to become easily distracted, and performance deteriorates. They may attend to the wrong cues, be unable to discriminate between which are relevant and irrelevant, or their attention may simply jump from one cue to another in the array of information available.

Imagery – definitions and types

Imagery has been defined by Block (1981) as the use of **visualisation** to imagine situations. Athletes who speak of visualisation, imagery or **mental**

practice are all referring to the process of creating an experience in the mind. Imagery can be used by sportspeople for a variety of purposes: to improve the performance of skills (known as mental practice), to increase self-confidence, to control arousal before performance, or to increase understanding or retention of information.

Two types of imagery have been identified, and you will see in the discussion which follows that sometimes both types are used:

- **internal imagery** is imagining yourself doing something, so you feel yourself performing, you experience being in the imagined situation
- **external imagery** is seeing yourself do something as though watching yourself on film, from the outside.

Theme link to Perspectives and Issues (**cognitive psychology**)

The topics of attention and imagery are part of the **cognitive approach** in psychology. The content of this chapter is an example. Attention relates to how we select incoming information; imagery relates to how we think about and retain information so that we can use it in the future. One way of understanding mental activity is to see the mind as a processor of information, hence the use of the term '**information processing approach**' to describe some of the models in cognitive psychology.

We have examined a brief description of the work on attention, noting the differences between selective attention and capacity theory. Once again arousal plays a part, causing attentional narrowing which in turn affects performance. If we cannot use automatic processing to reduce attentional demands, we may experience attentional overload, which also damages performance. However, the effects of arousal, and performance in general, can be altered by the use of imagery.

Section summary

Attention: measures, styles and strategies

MEASURING ATTENTION

Attention can be measured using behavioural, physiological and self-report methods, which are described below.

behavioural measures

Attention can be measured by using the probe technique to test reaction times. In this the participant is asked to perform a task such as sorting cards into piles. Whilst doing so they must also respond to a simple stimulus whenever it occurs, such as pressing a button when a buzzer is sounded. Research shows that participants who are not skilled at the motor task take longer to react to the buzzer than those who are skilled at the task. The conclusion is that the skilled performer has more attentional capacity available to notice and respond to the buzzer.

physiological measures

By using measures of arousal such as changes in blood pressure, heart or breathing rate, physiological research gains information about arousal levels and changes in attention. Details of **physiological measures** are given in Chapter 4 on arousal (p.54), which also examines the drawbacks of their use in a real sports setting. The athlete's awareness of the measuring equipment may itself affect levels of arousal, and thus affect the performance.

questionnaire

Questionnaires are less valuable as measures of attentional focus at a particular time (such as when performing a particular action) but more useful for identifying the tendency of the sportsperson to use particular styles, in other words for identifying an underlying trait.

An example is Nideffer's (1976) Test of Attentional and Interpersonal Style (TAIS). This is based on the two dimensions of broad/narrow and external/internal attentional focus, which are described in detail in the next section. The TAIS allows the researcher to identify the athlete's scores on six subscales, and from these scores to measure aspects of their attentional style. This is useful for matching the sportsperson to the most appropriate sport or position on the field, or to help them compensate for weaknesses.

ATTENTIONAL STYLE

We have already looked at attention in terms of the selection of relevant cues, and the term 'attentional style' refers to where that attention is focused within the environment – the attentional field. Sports psychologist Robert Nideffer (1976) proposed that attentional focus has two dimensions:

- **broad or narrow** – when it is broad the player can see several things at the same time, such as the position of key players when a ball is being dribbled up the field. When it is narrow the player is focusing on only one or two cues, as when the badminton player focuses on the opponent's racket.

- **external or internal** – external focus is directed outwards, towards the bounce of the ball or the position of a player. Internal attentional focus is directed towards the individual's own thoughts or feelings.

These two dimensions can be combined to give four attentional styles. These are shown, along with examples, in Table 8.1.

• **Table 8.1:** The four different attentional styles

	External	Internal
Broad	Broad-external (e.g. used to check positions of other players)	Broad-internal (e.g. used to plan tactics or strategy)
Narrow	Narrow-external (e.g. used to watch racket strike ball)	Narrow-internal (e.g. used to control anxiety)

Nideffer used these four styles in his development of the TAIS which, as we saw earlier, enables the researcher to test an athlete's attentional traits (which are fairly stable personality dispositions). The scores on the six subscales of the TAIS provide indications of either positive or negative attentional traits, as follows:

- **positive attentional traits** – athletes who have high scores on broad external and internal attentional focus, and are able to narrow their attentional focus when necessary, are **effective attenders**.
- **negative attentional traits** – athletes who are easily distracted, become overloaded with external and internal stimuli, and have a narrowed attentional focus which they are unable to broaden when necessary, are **ineffective attenders**.

A sportsperson can be classed as an effective or ineffective attender based on these scores. Those who are ineffective attenders will need help to switch their attention from broad to narrow when necessary. A player will be more effective if their attentional style suits their sport or skill. Hockey and rugby require a broad–external style and flexibility to change to the other styles, but gymnastics and golf require a narrow–internal style. This is a useful point for those who want to encourage others to participate in sports – think about their attentional style.

Nideffer (1980) has studied the effect of arousal on attention, and noted that increased arousal may result in the player scanning the attentional field less often and being taken by surprise, or failing to take in the full pattern of

• **Figure 8.2:** The value of a broad–external focus in basketball

play and missing opportunities to spot weaknesses or to score. He is also more likely to use his dominant attentional style rather than several attentional styles as the occasion demands.

ATTENTIONAL STRATEGIES

Knowledge about attention can be usefully applied by sportspeople, depending on the demands of their situation. Whilst focusing attention internally is valuable on some occasions, performers in sports involving considerable or prolonged physical stress need an external focus. Morgan (1978) distinguished between **associative** and **dissociative strategies**:

- **associaters** direct their attention internally, focusing on the body's feedback signals
- **dissociaters** direct their attention externally, blocking out feedback from the body.

Research on elite distance runners shows that they prefer to use the associative strategy when in competition, but the dissociative strategy when training. In a study of recreational runners, Wrisberg and Pein (1990) reported that less experienced runners tend to use the associative strategy. In contrast, more experienced runners use the dissociative strategy, which may enable them to push themselves harder.

Section summary

In this section we have seen how the ways of measuring attention can be used by researchers. We have seen how the two dimensions of attentional focus can be combined to produce four attentional styles, and noted the impact of arousal on attentional style. It should be possible to help the sportsman improve his performance by identifying whether he is an effective or ineffective attender and by using the most appropriate attentional strategy for his circumstances.

Imagery and mental practice

One of the uses of imagery is in mental practice, a technique used by sportspeople to improve their performance of skills. This is discussed in the final part of this section, but first we will consider other uses of imagery in sport.

INCREASING SELF-CONFIDENCE

Imagery allows the athlete to work through various strategies, to 'run through' a performance in her mind, perhaps by deciding how to cope with an opponent's tactics, or rehearsing what shots she will play. She can run through the situations which are potentially stressful without experiencing a negative outcome. This enables a player to feel prepared and so increases confidence.

CONTROLLING AROUSAL

Imagery is often used with relaxation techniques to reduce arousal. The athlete imagines the circumstances and feelings associated with being relaxed (often in combination with other techniques such as deep breathing) and becomes better able to cope with arousal or stress. David Hemery (1986) has described his loss of self-control on the warm-up track when he saw his main rival practising. He felt his throat tighten (a sign of anxiety) and used imagery to regain control:

I left my shoes off and taking easy strides ... took myself back to where I was running in a few inches of water on the firm sands of Powder Point Beach ... the sun was on my back and I felt the sensation of my body flowing with health and strength. The image was so strong that my mind was totally blank as to what I had just seen and I was back on to personal performance (p.118).

Arousal and emotions are closely related. Jackie Stewart (in Hemery, 1986) described how he used imagery prior to a Grand Prix race. He saw his emotional state as an over-inflated beach ball. During his emotional countdown towards the race time he would gradually deflate the ball until it was completely deflated and he was virtually emotionless.

UNDERSTANDING AND RETAINING INFORMATION

Information can be better understood and retained by creating a 'mind picture'. For example, if an athlete is told to 'visualise your limbs as cooked spaghetti', she is more likely to relax effectively than if simply told to 'relax'. A coach can talk to the athlete in terms which encourage her to create a mental image, such as suggesting that a sprinter 'explode' off the starting blocks.

MENTAL PRACTICE

Mental practice is the mental or cognitive rehearsal of a skill without actual physical movement. It can be used to experience many aspects of skill learning and sports performance, as David Hemery (1986) describes in his preparation for Olympic 400m hurdles:

> . . . apart from the physical practice, many more hours were spent mentally rehearsing the effort distribution, pace judgement, stride pattern and hurdling technique for a successful attempt (p.114).

David Hemery has also described the use of his kinaesthetic sense – the sense of the position of the limbs and their movement as he clears the hurdles. So, although we refer to imagery, we mean not only what we see in our minds, but also what we hear and smell, what we feel in our body and our emotions. Indeed, using imagery is more effective if it can be made more vivid by involving other senses – so Hemery could have created the feel of his heel hitting the ground, the sight of the next hurdle approaching and the sound of his own rhythm of steps, in order to make his imagery more intense.

Research suggests that when mental practice is combined with physical rehearsal of an action, this improves performance more than just physical rehearsal by itself. Why does mental practice have this effect? A number of explanations have been offered, which include the suggestions that mental practice:

* enables the performer to try out different strategies, to correct faults by replaying the skill correctly, to break down the performance of a skill into sub-routines.
* allows the sportsperson to perform without risk of public failure and avoids the arousal caused by performance in front of others.
* allows the athlete to suspend time and motion. For example, a gymnast can mentally practice take-off for a forward roll, can then focus on tucking in the limbs, then focus on the landing, taking as much time as is

necessary for each stage. The whole routine can then be mentally rehearsed as one unit.

- helps the athlete remember the skills learned during practice, for example during a rest period in training.
- activates the sportsperson so he or she is attending to the right cues, is prepared to expect certain stimuli, is prepared to respond to each of the stimuli and may be less likely to be disrupted if anxiety occurs. Some researchers, such as Suinn (1980), have proposed that mental practice causes slight activation of the neuromuscular system, so it is like a weak form of physical training. Research shows that there are tiny muscle movements during mental practice which reflect the movement of the muscles if they were actually performing the skill. According to this theory, if David Hemery had monitors attached to his leg and arm muscles when he was mentally rehearsing for his 400m hurdles, the monitors would show tiny muscle movements in his take-off leg as he imagined taking off.
- can be used during periods of injury to help athletes keep 'on top' of skills they are unable to perform physically.

Nideffer (1985) has noted that some sportspeople seem to use imagery skills naturally whereas others have great difficulty in developing them. He advises practising imagery when we are relaxed, without distraction and not close to performance. He also recommends practising external imagery by looking at ourselves from various angles as we perform the movement, and learning to use internal and external imagery interchangeably.

THE EFFECTIVENESS OF IMAGERY

Although the above quotations are what we call anecdotal evidence, research which provides experimental evidence has confirmed that approximately 90 per cent of elite athletes use some kind of imagery and attest to its value. Research suggests that the use of imagery is most effective:

- when performing skills requiring mostly cognitive components , according to Feltz and Landers (1983). Examples could be those skills which are under conscious control (because they are just being learned), those involving long sequences (such as gymnastics), or those involving decision-making and strategies (such as basketball). Imagery appears to have limited effect on skills with low cognitive requirements, such as weight-lifting.
- in enhancing the performance of experienced performers more than of novice performers. As an example, Issac (1992) used imagery questionnaires with expert and novice trampoliners. He reported that the

experts benefited from using imagery much more than the novices. It seems to help them refine skills and to make decisions or adjustments very rapidly. The novice, who does not know what the correctly performed skill feels like, cannot visualise performing it correctly.

Section summary   This section has considered some of the ways in which imagery can improve self-confidence, control arousal and help retain information. The value of mental practice in improving the performance of skills is well supported by evidence and it is widely used by elite athletes. However, to date, relatively little is known about how it actually generates these benefits.

KEY TERMS

associative strategies
attention
attentional capacity
attentional field
attentional focus
attentional narrowing
attentional style
automatic processing
capacity theory of attention
cognitive approach
dissociative strategies
effective attenders
external imagery
imagery
ineffective attenders
information processing approach
internal imagery
mental practice
overload
physiological measures
selective attention
visualisation

EXERCISE 1

Using the ideas on p.114, identify the tasks that will make demands on the attention of someone who is learning to play table-tennis.

EXERCISE 2

Working with a partner, choose two ways of measuring attention. Each of you write down two advantages and two disadvantages for each. Then get together and compare your answers.

EXERCISE 3

Think of a sports situation which you have found difficult, then describe one way in which imagery might have helped improve your performance.

ESSAY QUESTIONS

1. Describe the effects of arousal on attention, using your knowledge of psychological theory and evidence.

2. Explain why imagery seems to be most effective when it is used for skills with a high cognitive component.

3. What is the difference between external and internal imagery? Which do you think will be more effective for (a) a golfer practising putting and (b) two athletes practising a relay handover? Explain your answer.

Further reading

Cox, R. H. (1998) *Sport Psychology: Concepts and Applications* (4th ed). Boston, MA: WCB McGraw-Hill (Chapter 3 and 6).

Gill, D. L. (1986) *Psychological Dynamics of Sport*. Champaign, IL: Human Kinetics Publishers (Chapter 4).

Hardy, L., Jones, G. and Gould, D. (1996) *Understanding Psychological Preparation for Sport.* Chichester: John Wiley & Sons. (Chapter 7).

Horn, T. S. (Ed) (1992) *Advances in Sport Psychology*. Champaign, IL: Human Kinetics Publishers (Chapters 11 and 12).

Kremer, J. and Scully, D. (1994) *Psychology in Sport*. London: Taylor & Francis (Chapter 3).

Morris, T. and Summers, J. (Eds) (1995) *Sport Psychology – Theory, Applications and Issues*. Milton, Queensland: John Wiley & Sons (Chapters 3, 14 and 15).

Wann, D. L. (1997) *Sport Psychology*. Upper Saddle River, NJ: Prentice Hall, Inc. (Chapters 6 and 11).

Websites

http://www.mindtools.com/flowintro.html – describes how the brain responds to stimuli and discusses how this affects focus in sport situations

http://www.mindtools.com/imgintro.html – examples of the value and uses of imagery in a sports setting

http://www.brianmac.demon.co.uk – the use of mental imagery in relaxation techniques for sport performers

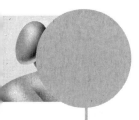

References

Arms, R. L., Russell, G. W. & Sandilands, M. L. (1979) Effects of viewing aggressive sports on the hostility of spectators. *Social Psychology Quarterly*, 42, 275–279.

Asken, M. J. (1991) The challenge of the physically challenged: Delivering sport psychology services to physically disabled athletes. *The Sport Psychologist*, 5, 370–381.

Bandura, A. (1977a) *Social learning theory.* Englewood Cliffs, NJ: Prentice Hall.

Bandura, A. (1977b) Self-efficacy: Toward a unifying theory of behavioral change. *Psychological Review,* 84, 191–215.

Bandura, A. (1982) Self-efficacy mechanism in human agency. *American Psychologist.* 37, 122–147.

Bandura, A., Ross, D. & Ross, S. (1961) Transmission of aggression through imitation of aggressive models. *Journal of Abnormal and Social Psychology*, 63, 375–382.

Barnett, N. P., Smoll, F. L. & Smith, R. E. (1992) Effects of enhancing coach–athlete relationships on youth sport attrition. *The Sport Psychologist,* 6, 111–127.

Baron, R. S. (1986) Distraction-conflict theory: Progress and problems. In L. Berkowitz (Ed), *Advances in experimental social psychology,* Vol.19. New York: Academic Press.

Berkowitz, L. (1969) *Roots of aggression.* New York: Atherton Press.

Berkowitz, L. (1972) Sports, competition, and aggression. In I. D. Williams & L. M. Wankel (Eds.), *Proceedings of the Fourth Canadian Psychomotor Learning and Sport Psychology Symposium* (pp.321–326) Waterloo, Ontario: University of Waterloo.

Berkowitz, L. & LePage, A. (1967) Weapons as aggression-eliciting stimuli. *Journal of Personality and Social Psychology,* 7, 202–207.

Berger, B. G., Friedmann, E. & Eaton, M. (1988) Comparison of jogging, the relaxation response, and group interaction for stress reduction. *Journal of Exercise Psychology*, 10, 4, 431–447.

Bird, A. M. (1977) Leadership and cohesion within successful and unsuccessful teams: Perceptions of coaches and players. In D. M. Landers & R. W. Christina (Eds.), *Psychology of motor behavior and sport* (Vol.2) Champaign, IL: Human Kinetics Publishers.

Bird, A. M. & Horn, A. (1990) Cognitive anxiety and mental errors in sport. *Journal of Sport and Exercise Psychology,* 12, 211–216.

Block, N. (Ed.) (1981) *Imagery*, Cambridge, MA: MIT Press.

Bowers, K. S. (1973) Situationalism in psychology: An analysis and a critique. *Psychological Review,* 80, 307–336.

Bredemeier, B. J. (1978) The assessment of reactive and instrumental athletic aggression. *Proceedings of the International Symposium on Psychological Assessment.* Neyanya, Israel: Wingate Institute for Physical Education and Sport.

Bredemeier, B. J. & Shields, D. L. (1986) Athletic aggression: An issue of contextual morality. *Sociology of Sport Journal,* 3, 15–28.

Burton, D. (1988) Do anxious swimmers swim slower?: Re-examining the elusive anxiety–performance relationship. *Journal of Sport and Exercise Psychology,* 10, 45–61.

Burton, D. (1989) Winning isn't everything: Examining the impact of performance goals on collegiate swimmer's cognitions and performance. *The Sport Psychologist*, 3, 105–132.

Carron, A. V. (1982) Cohesiveness in sports groups: Interpretations and considerations. *Journal of Sport Psychology,* 4, 123–138.

Carron, A. V. & Bennett, B.B. (1977) Compatibility in the coach–athlete dyad. *Research Quarterly,* 48, 671–679.

Cattell, R. B. (1965) *The scientific analysis of personality.* Baltimore: Penguin.

Chelladurai, P. (1978) A multidimensional model of leadership. Unpublished doctoral dissertation. University of Waterloo, Waterloo, Ontario.

Chelladurai, P. & Carron, A. V. (1983) Athletic maturity and preferred leadership. *Journal of Sport Psychology,* 5, 371–380.

Cherry, E. C. (1953) Some experiments on the recognition of speech, with one and with two ears. *Journal of the Acoustical Society of America,* 25, 975–979.

Christie, L. (1995) *To be honest with you.* London: Penguin.

Cooper, L. (1969) Athletics, activity, and personality: A review of the literature. *Research Quarterly,* 40, 17–22.

Costill, D. L., Thomas, R., Robergs, R. A., Pascoe, D., Lambert, C., Barr, S. & Fink, W. J. (1991) Adaptations to swimming training: Influence of training volume. *Medicine and Science in Sports and Exercise*, 23, 371–377.

Cottrell, N. B. (1968) Performance in the presence of other human beings: Mere presence, audience, and affiliation effects. In E. C. Simmell, R. A. Hoppe & G. A. Milton (Eds.) *Social facilitation and imitative behavior* (pp. 91–110) Boston: Allyn & Bacon.

Courneya, K. S. & Carron, A. V. (1991) Effects of travel and length of home stand/road trip on the home advantage. *Journal of Sport & Exercise Psychology,* 13, 42–49.

Cox, R. H. (1998) *Sport psychology: Concepts and applications* (4th ed) Dubuque, IA: Wm. C. Brown Communications.

Deci, E. (1975) *Intrinsic Motivation*, New York: Plenum Press.

Dollard, J., Doob, J., Miller, N., Mowrer, O. & Sears, R. (1939) *Frustration and aggression.* New Haven, CT: Yale University Press.

Edwards, J. (1979) The home field advantage. In J. H.Goldstein (Ed.) *Sports, games, and play: Social and psychological viewpoints.* Hillsdale, NJ: Halstead Press.

Eysenck, H. J. (1965) *Fact and fiction in psychology.* Harmondsworth: Penguin.

Eysenck, H. J. & Eysenck, S. B. G. (1975) *Manual of Eysenck personality questionnaire.* London: Hodder & Stoughton.

Fazey, J. & Hardy, L. (1988) The inverted-U hypothesis: a catastrophe for sport psychology? *British Association of Sports Sciences Monograph No.1.* Leeds: The National Coaching Foundation.

Feltz, D. L. & Landers, D. M. (1983) The effects of mental practice on motor skill learning and performance: A meta-analysis. *Journal of Sport Psychology,* 5, 25–57.

Fiedler, F. E. (1967) *A theory of leadership effectiveness.* New York: McGraw-Hill.

Fisher, A. C., Mancini, V. H., Hirsch, R. L., Proulx, T. J. & Staurowsky, E. J. (1982) Coach–athlete interactions and team climate. *Journal of Sport Psychology*, 4, 388–404.

Fodero, J. M. (1980) An analysis of achievement motivation and motivational tendencies among men and women collegiate gymnasts. *International Journal of Sport Psychology,* 11, 100–112.

Garcia, A. W. & King, A. C. (1991) Predicting long-term adherence to aerobic exercise: A comparison of two models. *Journal of Sport and Exercise Psychology,* 13, 4, 394–410.

Gill, D. L. (1980) Success–failure attributions in competitive groups: An exception to egocentrism. *Journal of Sport Psychology,* 2, 106–114.

Gill, D. L. (1986) *Psychological dynamics of sport.* Champaign IL: Human Kinetics Publishers.

Gill, D. L. & Deeter, T. E. (1988) Development of the SOQ. *Research Quarterly for Exercise and Sport*, 59, 191–202.

Gill, D. L. & Dzewaltowski, D. A. (1988) Competitive orientations among intercollegiate athletes: Is winning the only thing? *The Sport Psychologist*, 2, 212–221.

Gill, D. L., Gross, J. B. & Huddleston, S. (1983) Participation motivation in youth sports. *International Journal of Sport Psychology*, 14, 1–14.

Gould, D. & Weiss, M. (1981) The effects of model similarity and model task on self-efficacy and muscle endurance. *Journal of Sport Psychology*, 3, 17–29.

Greer, D. L. (1983) Spectator booing and the home advantage: A study of social influence in the basketball arena. *Social Psychology Quarterly*, 46, 252–261.

Gross, R. (1996) *Psychology: The science of mind and behaviour.* London: Hodder & Stoughton.

Halpin, A. W. (1966) *Theory and research in administration.* London: Macmillan.

Hemery, D. (1986) *Sporting Excellence.* Champaign, IL: Human Kinetics Books, A Division of Human Kinetics Publishers, Inc.

Hemphill, J. K. & Coons, A. E. (1957) Development of the leader behavior description questionnaire. In R. M. Stodgill & A. E. Coons (Eds.) *Leader behavior: Its description and measurement.* Columbus: Ohio State University Press.

Hersey, P. & Blanchard, K. H. (1969) Life cycle theory of leadership. *Training and Developmental Journal*, 23, 26–34.

Hill, G. (1998) *Advanced Psychology through Diagrams*. Oxford: Oxford University Press.

Horn, T. S. & Glenn, S. (1988) *The relationship beteween athletes' psychological characteristics and their preference for particular coaching behaviors.* Paper presented at the meeting of the North American Society for the Psychology of Sport and Physical Activity, Knoxville, Tn., USA.

Hull, C. L. (1951) *Essentials of behavior.* New Haven, CT: Yale University Press.

Issac, A. (1992) Mental practice – does it work in the field? *The Sport Psychologist*, 6, 192–198.

Jones, J. G. & Hardy, L. (1990) *Stress and performance in sport.* Chichester: John Wiley & Sons.

Jourden, F. J., Bandura, A. & Banfield, J. T. (1991) The impact of conceptions of ability on self-regulatory factors and motor skill acquisition. *Journal of Sport and Exercise Psychology,* 13, 213–226.

Kagan, A. (1975) Epidemiology, disease and emotion. In L. Levi (Ed), *Emotions, their parameters and measurement.* New York: Raven Press.

Kahneman, D. (1973) *Attention and effort.* Eaglewood Cliffs, NJ: Prentice Hall.

Kyllo, L. B. & Landers, D. M. (1995) Goal setting in sport and exercise: A research synthesis to resolve the controversy. *Journal of Sport & Exercise Psychology*, 17, 117–137.

Lacey, J. J. (1967) Somatic response patterning and stress: Some revisions of activation theory. In M. H. Appley & R. Trumbell (Eds) *Psychological stress: Issues in research.* New York: Appleton-Century-Crofts.

Landers, D. M., Qi, W. M. & Courtet, P. (1985) Peripheral narrowing among experienced rifle shooters under low and high stress conditions. *Research Quarterly for Exercise and Sport*, 56, 122–130.

Latané, B., Harkins, S. G. & Williams, K. D. (1980) Many hands make light work: Social loafing as a social disease. Unpublished manuscript. The Ohio State University, Columbus, Ohio.

Latané, B., Williams, K. D. & Harkins, S. G (1979) Many hands make light work: The causes and consequences of social loafing. *Journal of Personality & Social Psychology,* 37, 822–832.

Leonard, W. M. III (1989) The 'home advantage': The case of the modern Olympics. *Journal of Sport Behavior,* 12, 227–241.

Lepper, M. R. & Greene, D. (1975) Turning play into work: Effect of adult surveillance and extrinsic rewards on children's intrinsic motivation. *Journal of Personality and Social Psychology,* 31, 479–486.

Leith, L. M. & Taylor, A. H. (1990) Psychological aspects of exercise: A decade literature review, *Journal of Sport Behaviour, 13,* 4, 219–239.

Lewin, K., Lippitt, R. & White, R. (1939) Patterns of aggressive behaviour in experimentally created 'social climates'. *Journal of Social Psychology,* 10, 271–299.

Locke, E. A. & Latham, G. P. (1990) *A theory of goal setting and task performance.* Englewood Cliffs, NJ: Prentice Hall.

Locke, E. A., Shaw, K. M., Saari, L. M. & Latham, G. P. (1981) Goal setting and task performance: 1969–1980. *Psychological Bulletin,* 90, 125–152.

Lorenz, K. Z. (1966) *On aggression.* London: Methuen.

Martens, R. A. (1977) *Sport Competition Anxiety Test.* Champaign, IL: Human Kinetics Publishers.

Martens, R., Vealey, R. S. & Burton, D. (1990) *Competitive anxiety in sport.* Champaign, IL: Human Kinetics Books.

Maslow, A. (1954) *Motivation and personality.* New York: Harper & Row.

McClelland, D. C., Atkinson, J., Clark, R. & Lowell, E. (1953) *The achievement motive.* New York: Appleton-Century-Croft.

McNair, D. M., Lorr, M. & Droppleman, L. F. (1971) *Profile of Mood States Manual.* San Diego, CA: Educational and Industrial Testing Service.

Miller, N. E. (1941) The frustration–aggression hypothesis. *Psychological Review,* 48, 337–342.

Mischel, W. (1968) *Personality and adjustment.* New York: Wiley.

Morgan, W. P. (1974) Selected psychological considerations in sport. *Research Quarterly,* 45, 324–339.

Morgan, W. P. (1978, April) The mind of the marathoner. *Psychology Today,* 38–49.

Morgan, W. P. (1979) Prediction of performance in athletics. In P. Klavora & J. V. Daniel (Eds.) *Coach, athlete, and the sport psychologist* (pp.172–186) Champaign, IL: Human Kinetics Publishers.

Morgan, W. P. (1980) The trait psychology controversy. *Research Quarterly for Exercise and Sport,* 51, 50 –76.

Morgan, W. P., Brown, D. R., Raglin, J. S., O'Connor, P. J. & Ellickson, K. A. (1987) Psychological monitoring of overtraining and staleness. *British Journal of Sports Medicine,* 21, 3, 107–114.

Mosston, M. & Ashworth, S. (1986) *Teaching physical education.* Columbus, Ohio: Merrill Publishing Co.

Nideffer, R. M. (1976) Test of attentional and interpersonal style. *Journal of Personality and Social Psychology,* 34, 394–404.

Nideffer, R. M. (1980) The relationship of attention and anxiety to performance. In W. F. Straub (Ed.) *Sport psychology: An analysis of athlete behavior* (2nd ed.) Ithaca, NY: Mouvement Publications.

Nideffer, R. M. (1985) *Athlete's guide to mental training.* Champaign, IL: Human Kinetics Publishers.

Nisbett, R. E., Caputo, C., Legant, P. & Maracek, J. (1973) Behaviour as seen by the actor and as seen by the observer. *Journal of Personality and Social Psychology,* 27, 154–165.

Ogilvie, B. C. (1968) Psychological consistencies within the personality of high-level competitiors. *Journal of the American Medical Association*, 205, 780–786.

Orlick, T. (1978) *Winning through cooperation.* Washington, DC: Hawkins.

Oxendine, J. B. (1970) Emotional arousal and motor performance. *Quest,* 13, 23–30.

Rogers, C. R. (1961) On becoming a person. Boston: Houghton Mifflin.

Rotter, J. B. (1966) Generalised expectancies for internal versus external control of reinforcement. *Psychological Monographs,* 80 (1 Whole No. 609).

Sallis, J. F., Haskell, W. L., Fortmann, S. P., Vranizan, K. M., Taylor, C. B. & Solomon, D. S. (1986) Predictors of adoption and maintenance of physical activity in a community sample. *Preventive Medicine*, 15, 331–341.

Sallis, J. F. & Hovell, M. F. (1990) Determinants of exercise behavior. In K. B. Pandolf & J. O. Holloszy (Eds.) *Exercise and sport science reviews* (18, 307–330) Baltimore: Williams & Williams.

Schachter, S. & Singer, J. E. (1962) Cognitive, social and physiological determinants of emotional state. *Psychological Review,* 69, 379–399.

Schmidt, G. W., & Stein, G. L. (1991) Sport commitment: A model integrating enjoyment, dropout, and burnout. *Journal of Sport and Exercise Psychology*, 13, 3, 254–265.

Schwartz, B. & Barsky, S. F. (1977) The home advantage. *Social Forces*, 55, 641–661.

Secord, P. F. & Backman, C. W. (1964) *Social psychology.* New York: McGraw-Hill.

Seligman, M. E. P. (1975), *Helplessness: on depression, development, and death.* San Francisco: W. H. Freeman.

Silva, J. M. III (1980) Assertive and aggressive behaviour in sport: A definitional clarification. In C.H. Nadeau (Ed.) *Psychology of motor behavior and sport, 1979* (pp. 199–208) Champaign, IL: Human Kinetics Publishers.

Silva, J. M. III (1984) Personality and sport performance: Controversy and challenge. In J. M. Silva, III & R. S. Weinberg (Eds) *Psychological Foundations of Sport*. Champaign, IL: Human Kinetics Publishers.

Silva, J. M. III (1990) An analysis of the training stress syndrome in competitive athletics. *Journal of Applied Sport Psychology*, 2, 5–20.

Smith, R. E., Smoll, F. L. & Curtis, B. (1979) Coach effectiveness training: A cognitive–behavioural approach to enhancing relationship skills in youth sports coaches. *Journal of Sport Psychology,* 1, 59–75.

Smith, R. E., Smoll, F. L. & Hunt, E. (1977) A system for the behavioral assessment of athletic coaches. *Research Quarterly*, 48, 401–407.

Smith, R. E. & Smoll, F. L. (1984) Leadership research in Youth Sports. In J. M. Silva & R. S. Weinberg (Eds). *Psychological Foundations of Sport*. Champaign, IL. Human Kinetics Publishers.

Smith, R. E. & Smoll, F. L. (1990) Self-esteem and children's reactions to youth sport coaching behaviors: A field study of self-enhancement processes. *Developmental Psychology*, 26, 987–993.

Smoll, F. L. & Smith, R. E. (1989) Leadership behaviors in sport: A theoretical model and research paradigm. *Journal of Applied Social Psychology*, 19, 1522–1551.

Spence, K. W. (1956) *Behaviour theory and conditioning*. New Haven, CT: Yale University Press.

Spielberger, C. D. (1971) Trait-state anxiety and motor behaviour. *Journal of Motor Behavior* 3, 265–279.

Steiner, I. D. (1972) *Group processes and productivity*. New York: Academic Press.

Suinn, R. M. (1980), Body thinking: Psychology for Olympic champs. In R. M. Suinn (Ed.) *Psychology in sports: Methods and applications*. Minneapolis: Burgess Publishing Company.

Tajfel, H. (1970) Experiments in intergroup discrimination. *Scientific American*, 223, 96–102.

Tajfel, H. (Ed) (1978) *Differentiation Between Social Groups: Studies in the Social Psychology of Intergroup Relations*. London: Academic Press.

Triandis, H. C. (1990) Theoretical concepts that are applicable to the analysis of ethnocentrism. In R. W. Brislin (Ed.) *Applied Cross-Cultural Psychology*. Newbury Park, CA: Sage.

Tuckman, B. W. (1965) Developmental sequences in small groups. *Psychological Bulletin*, 63, 384–399.

Varca, P. E. (1980) An analysis of home and away game performance of male college basketball teams. *Journal of Sport Psychology*, 2, 245–257.

Vealey, R. S. (1986) Conceptualization of sport-confidence and competitive orientation: Preliminary investigation and instrument development. *Journal of Sport Psychology*, 8, 221–246.

Veroff, J. (1969) Social comparison and the development of achievement motivation. In C. P. Smith (Ed.) *Achievement-related motives in children* (pp. 46–101) New York: Russell Sage Foundation.

Vroom, V. H. & Yetton, P. W. (1973) *Leadership and decision making*. Pittsburgh: University of Pittsburgh Press.

Weinberg, R. S., Bruya, L. D. & Jackson, A. (1985) The effects of goal proximity and goal specificity on endurance performance. *Journal of Sport Psychology*, 7, 296–305.

Weiner, B. (1972) *Theories of motivation: From mechanism to cognition*. Chicago: Rand McNally.

Weiner, B. (1979) A theory of motivation for some classroom experiences. *Journal of Educational Psychology*, 71, 3–25.

Weiss, M. R. & Petlichkoff, L. M. (1989) Children's motivation for participation in and withdrawal from sport: Identifying the missing links. *Pediatric Exercise Science*, 1, 195–211.

Westre, K. R. & Weiss, M. R. (1991) The relationship between perceived coaching behaviors and group cohesion in high school football teams. *The Sport Psychologist*, 5, 41–54.

Williams, L. R. T. & Parkin, W. A. (1980) Personality profiles of three hockey groups. *International Journal of Sport Psychology,* 11, 113–120.

Woodcock, A. J. & Corbin, C. C. (1992) The effect of verbal feedback on intrinsic motivation and perceived competence of cricketers. *Research Quarterly for Exercise and Sport* (Abstract) Supplement to 63, A-83.

Wrisberg, C. A. & Pein, R. L. (1990) Past running experience as a mediator of the attentional focus of male and female recreational runners. *Perceptual and Motor Skills*, 70, 427–432.

Zajonc, R. B. (1965) Social facilitation. *Science,* 149, 269–274.

Zajonc, R. B. (1968) Attitudinal effects of mere exposure. *Journal of Personality and Social Psychology*, Monograph Supplement 9, Part 2, 1–27.

Zander, A. (1975) Motivation and performance of sports groups. In D. M. Landers (Ed.) *Psychology of sport and motor behavior II.* University Park, PS: Pennsylvania State University Press.

Zillman, D. & Bryant, J. (1974) Effect of residual excitation on the emotional response to provocation and delayed aggressive behaviour. *Journal of Personality and Social Psychology*, 30, 782–791.

Index